Tokyo Poetry Journal

Vol. 4 · Heisei Generations
Guest edited by Jordan A. Y. Smith

Advisory Board:

Rona Conti
Forrest Gander
Sam Hamill
Seiji Lippit
Sawako Nakayasu

Maureen Robertson
Jerome Rothenberg
Doug Slaymaker
John Solt
Keijiro Suga

Editor-in-chief
Taylor Mignon

Editor Emeritus
Barbara Summerhawk

Editor
Jeffrey Johnson

Japanese Poetry Editor
Jordan A. Y. Smith

Copy Editor
Simon Scott

Cover art by Akino Kondoh© (http://akinokondoh.com) courtesy of Mizuma Art Gallery (http://mizuma-art.co.jp).

Special Thanks to: Akino Kondoh, Mizuma Sueo and Osada Miho @ Mizuma Art Gallery, editorial assistants Jonas Engesvik, Alicja Strzałkowska, Dominika Izdebska, Adelina Torubara, Ádám Kertész, Dorina Kosztrics, and Ken Pacio.

Subscriptions available via bank transfer or international postal money order (sent to address below): ¥1500/issue or ¥2500/year for individuals, ¥2500/ issue or ¥3500/year for institutions. Make bank transfers to Japan Postal Savings: Japan Post Bank—c/o Jeffrey Johnson, Bank Code 10020, account #24951451. No personal checks please.

Submissions are accepted for issues on an ongoing basis. Email submissions are preferred. Please send either MS Word or PDF files (both if possible) in 11 pt. Times New Roman (unless typeface is important to your creative MO) w/ 1-inch margins top, bottom and sides and smart quotes to: <topojo2015@gmail.com> For translations, include the original and confirm author permissions.

Send postal mail submissions and subscription payments to:

Tokyo Poetry Journal c/o Taylor Mignon
1-417, 4-13-24 Shirahata, Minami-ku
Saitama-shi, Saitama-ken 336–0022 Japan

Our old URL: http://topojo2015.wix.com/topojowebsite
Blog URL: http://tokyopoetry.com
Find us on Facebook (QR right):
https://www.facebook.com/tokyopoetryjournal
https://soundcloud.com/youtube-topojo

Printed by Printed Matter Press
Printed in Japan ISBN 978-1-933-60643-9

"I Am Forgetting Something"

I am forgetting something

Something vital I've forgotten

The moment I recall just what it is,

I may cease to be the me I've come to know

– Michiyama Rain

TABLE OF CONTENTS

Heisei Generations:
Poetic Function and Anti-Function
in an Era of Abdication

Jordan A. Y. Smith

Heisei generations invites a double interpretation—the generations of poets who entered the expanding world of Japanese poetry during the current Heisei Era (1989 to date), and what these poets have *generated* during this time: the generations of the Heisei generations. Often referred to as the "lost decades," the name Heisei (平成) derives from classical Chinese history texts and denotes the universalization of peace. So it began on an optimistic note, but the economy simply would not dance. Enter an era marked by an historic national refusal to procreate, an economy that generates disappointment in terms of macroeconomic benchmarks and microeconomic microaggressions, and a government that turns to superflat pop arts for international image-doctoring while it tries to eat the humanities for breakfast. Hell—for the first time in history, even the era's eponymous emperor wants to abdicate.

So what's up, Poetry? This volume brings together some three-dozen Heisei poets and translators for a verbal sketch of the era. Roman Jakobson famously discussed language in terms of *functions*, describing in a 1958 address the *poetic function* as having a "focus on the message for its own sake," language that calls attention to its own medium, its own interventions into the everyday idiom and the flow of meaning. If Jakobson's assertion puts poetry and linguistics in dialogue, this special issue of *ToPoJo* witnesses the *poetic function* more in anthropological terms.

In Tokyo today, poetry is certainly distancing itself from everyday language, but sometimes through its presentation rather than through the written word—distancing its practitioners at the social level from an "everyday" world increasingly dominated by the monopolization of time by regimes of work. Poetry in Japan is increasingly a mode that "poets" shift into by inhabiting performative spaces, ones where difference and anti-function—the active, willful rejection of work as a regime—are celebrated. And many of our readers will surely agree: work in Japan is a tricky concept.

In the rationally globalized economy, "work" is often associated with regimes of *techne*, or an all-encompassing efficiency, which Jacques Ellul critiqued thoroughly in his opus, *The Technological Society*. Work in Japan is not always about output, but about the unspectacular yet communally witnessable sacrifice of time itself. Work is not necessarily efficiency or productivity. This creates a rather unique opportunity for poetry as resistance in Japan—it can reject work as a colonization of time and body without rejection of the notion of productivity that actually, one might argue, has nothing to do with "work" as a regime of *techne*. *Otsukaresama-deshita*—that oft-used phrase once translated with tongue-in-cheek literality by Karen Yamashita as "you are honorably tired"—refers only to the mythical accrual of fatigue, not about having done well or accomplished something. Hence poets can reject regimes of control yet use poetry freely and guiltlessly in commissioned work for various industries (engineering companies, perfume campaigns, beer can designs, etc.).

This has become in Heisei an important way of rejecting the nasty business of soul crushing and frequently pointless labor, while creating soft power for poetry. The world of poetry is a space of anti-function, breaking out of normative schedules and the demand for the fatal banality of ritual language. In Japan, the Imperial Household Agency, in one form or another, has controlled ritual and image surrounding the emperor for some 1300 years—now the Heisei ritual regulators have had to dust off the rulebooks on imperial abdication. This is the first imperial reign where the emperor's influence and the meaning of this era's name has been usurped not by a shogun but by an economic condition, where it has been overshadowed not by the horrific, spectacular monster of war, but by the nebulous and insipid fears of a population in decline—both as a demographic fact and a sociopsychological deterioration.

The economic downturn has led to increasing pressures to work harder and spend more, both of which have brought highly questionable economic stimulus and unquestionable alienation in a wide variety of relationships. To buzzwordize through the common mass media assessments: it's a terrain where *otaku* play, *hikikomori* hide, *sōshoku-danshi* masturbate the nation into *shōshika*, and *shin-sotsugyōsei* do *shūshoku-katsudō* in conformity suits, hopefully join legions of once-iconic *sarariiman* who work *zangyō* until they submit to *karōshi* or end it all with a *jinshin-jiko*, and senior citizens who embody the specter of *kōreika* redeem themselves by braving the *hōshanō* in Fukushima to keep a ruined land productive. I could go on.

In the arts, many seek to express and resist the matrix of woes that has become synonymous with the era of abdication. Given the determining primacy of economics, poetry currently provides a space of resistance, one where within the din of non-conformity, the generations of poets who "debuted" since 1989 have found interesting ways not only of furthering poetry's range of techniques, political approaches and aesthetics, but of surviving the multivalent losses of the so-called "lost decades."

Akino Kondoh's cover art for this volume similarly embodies this—a young woman in near grayscale shelters from the rain under her bright red umbrella, her imagination apparent behind her serene expression, transforms the rain into colorless but technically brilliant butterflies. The butterflies, which also project onto the girl's hair, appear to be in flight, but are all actually viewed as though framed for viewing: the dullness of the climate is transformed not into natural beauty but into a fantasy based on taxidermy, the desire to preserve for observation (see Kanie Naha's poem on it below). Yet the image is seductive and nostalgic, it feels like a still from classic cinema—a stunningly crisp black-and-white eddy set-off by the bold fabric of an accessory. Red is a choice, and so is butterfly hair if you inhabit augmented reality.

Poetry as augmenting a rainy reality, not only an aesthetic defense. Many of the poems herein go sociopolitical, with Oshima Takeo's working class parable of crabs working in a warehouse for canned crabmeat and Ishiwata Kimi's terrifyingly ambiguous image of either a protest suicide or a mother shedding her domestic duties. Both these poets inhabit the world of performance more so than printed poetry, one with long traditions in modern poetry circles up and down the Japanese archipelago—carried on still in the famously shamanistic "happenings" of Yoshimasu Gōzō or jazz improv readings of Shiraishi Kazuko. Heisei poets continue in this avant-garde vein, but this new avenue concludes performances with score cards: Ishiwata made the 2017 national finals in Poetry Slam Japan, and Oshima won the competition in 2016, continuing on to Paris to represent Japan in the Poetry Slam World Cup.

Nakauchi Komoru earned this honor in 2017 after edging out yours truly in the very last performance of the finals—the fact that I made it so far was certainly testimony to Japanese poetry's welcoming attitude toward "outsiders." Fie on Endo Shūsaku's *Silence*, plenty of foreign seeds grow here—just ask Tian Yuan, Jeffrey Angles, or Andrew Campana, part of a growing group of foreign writers composing poetry in Japanese (their Japanese poems are included here, as are translations by Angles of Osaki Sayaka and by Campana of several poets he introduces in a dynamic essay preceding them). Tian has been awarded the "Mr. H" Prize for eroticism in poetry, while Angles joined Hideo Levy in receiving this year's Yomiuri Prize for Literature. Angles commented recently in an interview with super-translator Shibata Motoyuki for *Gendai-shi Techō* (May

2017) that exophonic writers gain from writing in another language, equipped with a different "clay" from which to shape their works. For Angles, the materiality of the language and its culture determines the quality and form of the poetic ware.

The same may be said of the performative venue—the atmosphere of recital bears a receptive spore that poets can sense in advance. They write with the knowledge that their voice and gestures, the lighting, dramatic pauses, the audience's response, will all be key ingredients. Performance oriented poetry can lie lifeless on the page, just as print-oriented poetry can go fish-out-of-water, parched and flopping in the limelight. This debate is at the heart of a new manga by Enokiya Katsumasa, *Mitsuko's Poem: High School Girl x Poetry Recital Battle* (©Shogakukan 2017), where the protagonist defiantly cries, as she graffitis her poem in lipstick on the teacher's face: "Being written on paper means nothing—if it's not *read*, it ain't *poetry*!" (See image right.) The process of becoming a poet is based on public performance in competitions rather than by erudite study in homage to the greats—so asserts Enokiya's Chapter 3, "A Poet Is Born in the Ring" (see image on the next page), and so affirms a growing community of poets in Japan linked ever more closely with their international counterparts. Thanks in large part to the efforts of Murata Katsuhiko, founder of Poetry Slam Japan, and the ongoing poetic diplomacy of past national representatives to Paris, slam poets from around the world have been making more frequent visits to Tokyo as a result (one love, Zohab!).

Even traditional forms like *tanka* have turned populist in language and theme. Venerable journals like Kadokawa's *Tanka* have devoted a special issue to "Considering Heisei Era

Tanka" (平成短歌の考察, 2017, vol. 64, no. 5), with articles like Tanioka Aki's "What the Bubble [Economy] Gave *Tanka*," and a special section on poets born in the first year of the Heisei Era (1989). Another, *Tanka Kenkyu-sha*, runs an award for *tanka* criticism, recently given to by Kajiwara Saiko's piece on orality (more precisely: *oralization* 口語化) in *tanka*, both in the way the poems are written and delivered, or on psychological issues that have become commonplace, such as Takahashi Keisuke writing on depersonalization (離人症), a state wherein one loses connection not only to society but to one's own body and feelings. Noguchi Ayako, included here in Nihei Chikako and Andrew Houwen's lucid translations, manifests Heisei *tanka* in many ways, with one verse expressing the paradox of a subject seeking the right emoji to describe being on a break at work—just as her break ends.

This turn toward current concerns and language has also hit free verse print poetry, often through the avenue of technopopulist social media. Many have pointed out how sites like Twitter and Facebook lend themselves to brevity, with a subsequently natural affinity to poetry. In the introduction to his book, *These Things Here and Now: Poetic Responses to the Disasters of March 11, 2011* (Josai University Press, 2016), Angles discusses poet Wagō Ryōichi, whose tweets following the earthquake brought the experience to followers in poetic detail. It was also a moment when poetry in Japan became less hermetic, more accessibly immediate.

This special issue includes some works of what might be considered populist poetry, even if it is for a "dysfunctional" or anti-functional populace. Saihate Tahi for one revels in a kind of post-love epoch of humanity, one marked in the visual arts by the group Chim↑Pom, with their "Love Is Over" project. More than a glorying in polyamorous liberation, her poetry is hauntingly comfortable with what I would call a 1-99 degree Celsius hate—one that doesn't quite freeze or boil, but ranges close to both extremes at times. Indifference moderates antipathy into apathy, but there is something oddly free. In the new film based on Saihate's collection, *The Night Sky Is Always the Highest Density Blue*, everyday language somehow finds a way to inhabit a defiant new everydayness, rejecting realism like Brecht did, but shaping a new and expanded emotional realism in the process. It's as though his *verfremdungseffekt* has settled quietly into reality, and Saihate is reorienting her thoroughly alienated readers. On her website (tahi.jp), her works reincarnate as electronic poetry, which can be invitingly interactive in the vein of OuLiPo's works such as Raymond Queneau's *A Hundred Thousand Billion Poems* (1961), or as antagonistic as a Space Invaders parody in which her poems invade like an alien fleet and the reader must blast them to smithereens

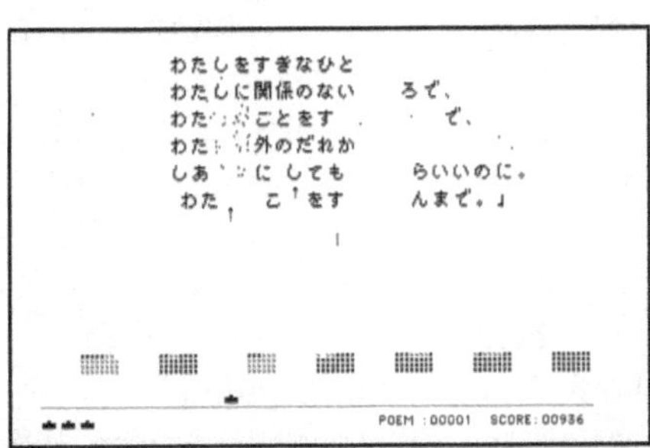

before being overrun (as in the image above). In need of some fake eyelashes? Her website also provides some patterns you can cut out and paste on—spelling out messages of love, hate, and everything between.

One can't really say "don't worry," but "be happy" does fall on many an open ear. This volume could be considered in some ways the poetic companion to recent academic volumes like *Happiness and the Good Life in Japan*, or *Life Course, Happiness and Well-being in Japan* (both edited by Wolfram Manzenreiter and Barbara Holthus). These collections, like

ToPoJo volume 4, consider happiness from a variety of angles, definitions, and subject positions. We would do well to remember that in recent years, the same authors who brought us the wildly popular *The Courage to Be Happy* (幸せになる勇気) had previously brought us the even more wildly popular *The Courage to Be Hated* (嫌われる勇気). These two books of Adlerian psychology from Kishimi Ichirō and Koga Fumitake hint at a sad truth: courage is a prerequisite for being happy and being hated to the extent that one dwells in a world where happiness demand exceeds happiness supply. Macroeconomics tells us that in such a situation, happiness goes at an increasing premium. Poetry then might have a solution in its quantum economics, with its string theory vibrations, its wave-particle duality.

If that is the case, then the solution is in your hands—or at least a map to the solutions. By introducing a host of "new" poets to the Anglophone world here, this volume seeks to signpost where poetry is happening, or rather *around whom* it is happening. Yes, there are young giants of literary recognition here—multiple literary award winners like Saihate Tahi, Hachikai Mimi, Misumi Mizuki, Fuzuki Yumi, Nagae Yūki, Kanie Naha, Ōsaki Sayaka, Akegata Misei—and also giants of the stage, mentioned above in my discussion of poetry slams. But there are many more who would need to be included for this to be a full overview of the present era of Japanese poetry. (I should reveal that one selection criterion was that the poet *not* have a solo collection out in English—the goal was to expand the translationscape.) Heisei poets have generated new language through a kind of technocreolization, but their re-socialization of poetry is also a return to the roots of collaborative poetry, celebratory moments, and profound reflection.

It is a world that in the past year also lost two greats of Japanese and world poetry whom I'd like to mention—Ōoka Makoto (1931-2017) pioneered a modern return to the *renshi*, bringing in many major figures in world poetry for collaborative poetic experiences, and Burton Watson (1925-2017), legendary translator of too many great works of Chinese and Japanese literature to name. Watson translated this now globally famous first line of *Tales of the Heike*, "The bells of the Gion monastery in India echo with the warning that all things are impermanent." The Heisei Era affirms this fact of impermanence, but with an air that the tragedy is not so much in the impermanence itself as in what is done, or not done, within the brief span of existence. Thank you for taking time from your own brief existence to let poetry work on you, to let these Heisei poets share how they create *heisei* in and through their lines. If you haven't had the chance to join us for the era-defying scenes of poetry here, then let this volume be a draft of our calling card.

Warm thanks to the brave and patient Editors and Board at ToPoJo, and to the poets, translators, poet-translators, and editorial assistants involved in creating this volume. As Michiyama Rain writes in the epigraph, there is surely something I'm forgetting... All errors are ultimately my own.

–JS

Butterfly   **Minamikawa Yuko**
蝶   南川優子

In the early summer afternoon
I open a window.
Sunlight cuts into a sitting room and
shoots my mobile next to a fruit basket.
The phone trembles like cold fingertips.
Are you Mrs Minamikawa?
This time of day, it must be a cold call.
I stay quiet.
A low male voice speaks into my ear
like blood seeping through a handkerchief.
He is trying to sell something useless.
If I hang up, he'll probably ring me again.
I throw the mobile on my sofa and
avert my eyes to a gerbera
on the windowsill.

A white butterfly flutters into the room
and perches on the pink petals.
She sniffs the pollen and flies to the sofa.
He is muttering how useful what he is selling is.
She perches on the mobile,
being attracted to his voice.
When he finally mentions the name of the product,
She wraps the holes on the receiver
with her wings.

His voice becomes choky and
his words break apart.
The butterfly will not move.
I sit on the sofa and put my ear on it.
His panting vibrates through my ear to my spine
and fades out like bubbles of beer.

When it becomes quiet at the other end,
the butterfly raises her wings,
kisses 1 to 0 on the keypad
and flies away.

Examination   Minamikawa Yuko
検査   南川優子

When an apple is rolling down a street
in this town
we become vigilant
as it is too fresh.
It could be a bomb.
Since that autumn afternoon
when the wedding cake exploded
on the moment it was cut
every product in shops
should go through examination
before being sold.

Aren't these kidney beans bullets?
Aren't these strawberries artificially red?
Won't this Barbie doll become violent?
Isn't this rose stalk embroidered
on the cardigan a detonating fuse?

By the time we purchase the products
food is stale, clothes are grimy.

We eat and wear lifeless things
day after day.
When we see living creatures
our eyes brighten up.

When a fluffy Maltese dog passes by
children fight to stroke her.
When dandelions open by the roadside
adults caress them with their fingers.
When we see attractive men and women
we jump at them to kiss.

The examiners begin to suspect
that the freshest thing in this town
might be a human being.

From tomorrow, they will give us
a regular check
to be sure we are not explosive.
We cannot walk in the town
with our heads high
until we are approved safe
after waiting in a long queue.

Editor's Note: Minamikawa's poems were written originally in
Japanese and translated by the author.

Anthropoets
詩人類

Kuwahara Takiya
桑原滝弥

Violence is right.
Discrimination is right.
Abuse is right.
Rape is right.
Robbery is right.
Murder is right.
War is right.
Suicide is right.

Draw a ○ next to any of the above you think are truly right.

Everyone,
People around the world:
Recklessly dub yourselves poets
And settle this once and for all.

– Translation by Jordan A. Y. Smith

On the Brink of Life   Kuwahara Takiya
生き際について   桑原滝弥

My child,
You have been born
You may not have wanted to be born, but
Here you are, in this world

My son,
What kind of world do you see?
Is the wind blowing there?
Are your tears as young as we'd expect?

My daughter,
Can you hear my voice?
Perhaps someday you'll come to resent it
And will come to love someone

Mischief-maker,
Don't you cry
If you just can't hold back, do it under darkness
But definitely never so that you feel soothed

Tomboy,
Wounds are good things
Shake hands with cruelty itself
Become lovely and save it

Lost child,
Are the flowers in bloom?
Are the birds in song?
Do you reject the way things are, yield to wrath and tear them
apart?

Unknown child,
I'm sorry
But you're not mistaken
Do not die

Abandoned child,
Thank you
You are forever right
Live!

All children,
Put roots into Earth and revere the Sky
Face the ocean and scream
Scatter your aim every which-way and encounter whom you will

Lonely child,
Laugh
Exult in your solitude
And thus remain connected to everything

Oh, Child,
Oh, Life,
Oh, Spirit,
May you shine

Child of Light,
Congratulations on being born
I will forever be by your side
Goodbye

See you again—soon!

– Translation by Jordan A. Y. Smith

Fretless   **Misumi Mizuki**
フレットレス   三角みづ記

In a garden of summer,
Plants do appear to enjoy themselves
But that's nothing more than description

Wield though I might
Words free of barriers
At times I would still draw your anger

In a garden of summer,
The sun's rays gently
Burn

As though remarking, *Sure is hot today*
I water the plants

Though I should be able
To wield words free of barriers
Your anger aroused
You feign sleep

Before the water dries up
I prepare breakfast
In the flow before it boils
Thinking up new words again
Thinking up new words that are not poetry.

– Translation by Jordan A. Y. Smith

Splashdown   Misumi Mizuki
着水   三角みづ記

When I don't want to cry
But fake cry anyway:
Soul for sale.
With you   the change so fast, that
I quickly forget

From forest to village   to sea   to sky
The one who chooses

These ever changing names   Is me.

Both living and dying
The one who chooses
Is me
Above the clouds
Unchanging temperature
Humidity
Sunset blazes into a ring, recoils

When I didn't want to cry
But fake cried anyway:
I remember it happening too quickly

The sold soul,
Sinks into deepest beauty
Casts itself into night
Back and forth
Mute
Under guise of tranquility,
Straight afterward,
I repeat the choice:
I don't want to cry
Yet cry

                                   – Translation by Jordan A. Y. Smith

Tower   **Kanie Naha**
塔   カニエ・ナハ

People being born
Do not exist
Appoint a single day of silence
That which I remember,
I will retain until this coming August.
To feel fear
In another land
Near my hometown
I've always bent my ears to people's tales,
In a birth
Close to the profound end
Of my own memories,
I was there, couldn't leave
Territory, same name as the House
Various things
For the local god
Silently
I was listening to the fluttering wind
Clouds from ancient times
That intent called (the wind's drift)
Yielding to it,
A tree with that newborn purity,
Like that bird that has come now to your garden,
preserves its own immaculate state
Not sullying the flames
Searching the world for
A flame like itself
Eulogy in blood
Its thickness
Severed from humanity,
To build a valley,
Or to purify,

Through its descent,
Once abundant time gradually shortens
In the night, your forest
Moves without sound,
An eternal forgetting
Upon your tiny
Collection of all days,
Raining down moderately
Insects in the night, burning
To cultivate the friendship,
When born,
The people lifted voices of prayer,
Waving
Small leaves
The departing day
Carries on the long-ago darkness

– Translation by Jordan A. Y. Smith

Taxidermy   Kanie Naha
剥製   カニエ・ナハ

Affixed on the wall
Of my heavy eyelids:
Two dearly-departed horses,
In supremely intimate words,
Space of fancy,
Drifting through alarm clock and sleep and dreams
One after another, faithfully,

Reflected out to the very edges,
Flowing through the grove
Not so much accuracy as
Perhaps, within a so-called landscape
When their reception attunes to homesickness,
Standing on the bank of the racing river,
Oh, horses,
When you first visited from earth,
Aware of your derivation,
Your origins, you alighted on the station where I was;
Being that forest
On that very first day,
Soon enough, traveling a ghostlike world,
A house in the heart
At a touch,
It became a single
Decryption key,
Listening to the faint music,
For a moment, I
Visited a hospital
The black hairs on people's haggard faces
Rushed ever eastward skirting the pine forest,
With reminiscences, pushing ever forward
The waiting people long vanished,
Into the sea of humanity once more,
Unforeseen,
Through unknown means,
Within the well-remembered *monogatari*,
In the two paintings on the right,
Genesis of something called the ocean
Which I have yet to touch
Gentle, abundant time,
As of yet, as a horse, reaches the next world
Light floating near a scent
Non-existent in this world,

Conspicuously bright,
Its origins, still a swampy terrain
We vanish from reality
How late you are
No future, no past,
Under the ashes
Made into a timekeeper,
The remaining marshland
These phonemes have an
Immediate presence, when in my hand, white
Characters for *return* are scrawled,
Packaging of the voice,
Perhaps the very first
Roots of seedlings
The moon hangs suspended
In the cove within me, this
Drifting
The final name,
Perhaps water sounds,
I am called
Linked by chance
To the sea of that name,
Standing in a forest like night,
They drift to sleep again,
waiting for the next one to fall

– Translation by Jordan A. Y. Smith

Night of the Yukar   **Nagae Yūki**
ユーカラの夜   永方佑樹

≪tan θ + sin θ≫

Up in deepened sky of carbon
From the fringes of the Milky Way
Amethysts
Mimic zodiac figures as they come,
Star-cries for companions, blazing down:
Night of the *yukar*

People of this world—*kanna-mosir*
Dream of the next—*pokna-mosir*

Under the red oxide roofs,
Summer insects manufactured from thin silver
Emit quavering voices
Limbs soaked in the dark carbon night
Deep beneath eyelids,
Carving sounds of a clock wound in reverse
A torrent of sunlight

At that point

Bay leaf aroma from a motley knoll of roses
Sagittaria's rank luxury in pond water
Its bed a brocade of shed *koi* scales,
Stiff glossed in gelatin,
When it shines in wind-polished multicolor cellophane,
Harmonies from foreign deities
Spill translated rays round the enamel,
Then into the landscape
Fade in unison

Faint winkings of Sirius
From a flickering galaxy,
Moonlight warps, entangled in magnetism

Slathered buttery lethargy
The summer night begins to hum out a *yukar*
People of this world—*kanna-mosir*
Dream of the next—*pokna-mosir*

– Translation by Jordan A. Y. Smith

Note: A *yukar* is an Ainu saga. In one understanding of Ainu cosmology,
kanna-mosir designates the world of above ground, while *pokna-mosir*
designates the underworld.

Misty Spring Dawn   Nagae Yūki
はるけぶり   永方佑樹

《cosθ》

People   and   things   too, drunken,   dreams   as one,
   doze off in the dawn,
Howling wind quieted, faint   warm   weak
Odor of fermenting mash   breaking down
Peeling off one   layer of dead night at a time,
   in the smoldering omen
Dreams, shallowing out,
Trailing constricted shadow puppets,

Spill to the outside   and stride off.

Roadside. In the thinning dark of predawn,
Steel blue timber trees stand in unison   line up,
In the entangled branch tips of their mutual   differences
Bundles of pale flowers sag heavily   shine
Fireglow. Smoking   flowerglow softly emits
    peeled away scents
Traced in vaguely   wandering warmth, steadily buried.
Dulled   petals fray, brushing branches as they detach,
Choking on   the flowerglow.

Dimming out   buried in gloom, spun from the brief intervals,
Were   these blue quaking objects. Leaving them quietly behind,
A dream with fluffy gait   glitters through gloom   treading
the spring haze   pale   slumber bubbling over sleep
  with slight   hand movements
It pushes   right through.

Eyelids, alleviation.
With lips faintly parted   imbibe vestiges of dreamlight
Deep in the chest   alleviation ripples. Lights splash   disperse
Awakening   loosening.

                              – Translation by Jordan A. Y. Smith

**Listening to the Lovers'
Visit in the Morning Rain**
朝の雨に恋人のおとないを聞く

Akegata Misei
暁方ミセイ

Out of that dense growth, last night's
Thought remains but as a trace
Over there in that green patch
It was hit by a bright rain
For some time now
My muddied body
Was but a swirling dream
Turned to sentiment
In the end it had a slight feverishness
Descending deep
Reaching back several hundred years
A spring rain
Wetting the samurai's topknot
A dove came down from the mountain
Warmed beneath the wetted feathers
It's over ... quite over
It says in a mumbling chirp

– Translation by Jeffrey Johnson

Vision of Nagano
長野幻視

Akegata Misei
暁方ミセイ

A cold sun got even darker and weaker
I saw a gentle and smoky shadow flowing.
On the mountain this weather goes on and on,
the snow covered field turns dark and yellow,
and then sunlight leaked through like a thin breath.
The snow is frozen and blue
frost covered trees stand frozen as if a tribe.
Woods.
Branches hung with red and blue ornaments.
Those branches absorb the feeble sun,
sparkling light shows no hurry,
light that brings to mind winters' past,
within the blue shadow cast by
a monk walking in mediation
in that moment
in his heavy steps one after the other the melt begins

– Translation by Jeffrey Johnson

Saihate Tahi・最果タヒ

Translations by Jordan A. Y. Smith

The night that anyone who wants me to live
Disappeared   in the kitchen
I opened the refrigerator   and chugged down every drop of
milk left
In a world where there is no one who wants me to live
Now too a mother cow   is giving her milk to her child
I don't believe in some kind of universal love for all
But the fact that I can faintly believe   in a love someone gives
to another
Is probably because I had a mother

Cold Milk Poem   Saihate Tahi
つめたい牛乳の詩   最果タヒ

∞

Music kills me.
Kills youth.
Someday, I will come to resent it,
Even though I know this, I walk right in front of the explosive
sound
The sound,
Strips off and blows away these dust-like things,
Which alone were my everything. The music of dead people,
kills me.
That from here on to eternity,
They will never love me—that thought just barely keeps me
alive.

Record Poem   Saihate Tahi
レコードの詩   最果タヒ

∞

I have this I wanna die, I wanna disappear,
I only want to go to an aquarium feeling, and
It's time to go walk around town. Christmas, illumination.
The world seems to have nothing to do with me, such a bright,
cheerful era.
I should exist, though I feel like I don't.
I'm walking, though I feel like I'm not.
I have this I wanna die, I wanna disappear,
I only want to go to an aquarium,
Just for some bubblegum-like misery, for me, there is no need to
die.
Hiding my mouth, hiding my nose
Just got to slip from the world's gaze
In this easy suicide

Mask Poem   Saihate Tahi
マスクの詩   最果タヒ

∞

Whenever someone beautiful is nearby, it makes me look dirty,
So I want you to be dirty, and that emotion is called love, I hear
News of a person's death   a mosquito flying by
Humans telling tales of love
Can't control their urge to make excuses for it.
That voice saying, "Die!"—please let me record it.

Cassette Tape Poem   Saihate Tahi
カセットテープの詩   最果タヒ

∞

Love Letter   Saihate Tahi
恋文   最果タヒ

When Death wells up, on the raindrop above his head, a magpie
comes to rest, the tiny patter of footsteps, amidst the most
boisterous funeral, without anyone ever noticing. It's always
noisy around Death, an uproar. The crisscrossing of coarse
particles of conversations, mouths clammed up like those truly
close to the dead.
In the center of eternal silence.
Can't say "love."
Can't say "dream."
In some distant place, once again fireflies, are shining,
delighting.
Maybe like in some hot springs town.
Not a single one of us knows how to talk about this, and
someday enveloped in Death's approach, we sleep.
Before saying I want to be loved, I want to inform you in
whispers that I wanted to live, I want you to live. You're the
only person I know. Your breath, your pulse, to be forever tied
to this I have idly prayed. Dreadful, isn't it? Deep desire.
Though I knew someday I would surely be betrayed, I will never
forgive your death.

*Note: Some of Saihate's poems are positioned with the titles
following the poems, as per the author's original layout.*

Hu-hu-hu   **Tian Yuan**
フフフ   田原

*How this chuckle travels across national borders, I don't
know. I don't know how it reaches my ear, whether
through an undersea cable or a satellite in space. After all,
I should be grateful for this era.*

Hu-hu-hu   the hint of someone chuckling
She lives at the foot of Mt. Taishan
I have never met her
Though we were supposed to be introduced
She did not keep her promise
So our paths never crossed
But I've forgiven her
After all—that day was the memorial service at her family's
  home
And she was put in charge of chores serving her father helping
  at home
Only after she had sent me a thick pile of poetry and prose
Did I learn   that her gynecologist's assurance about her
  having a healthy uterus
Led her to live footloose
With regrettable habits ingrained

She grew up at her grandma's home
Perhaps she picked up bad habits then
At school age   for instance
She stuck around the school gate
And entered the school grounds jumping over the fences like a
  thief
Now near the decisive age of forty   for instance
She remains in a single pad of irregular life
Where dawns and dusks intermingle
And the sun and moon came and went carefree in her dreams

She was born with migraines
When the pain hit sweat bubbled out on her forehead
Bulging blue veins crawled like earthworms
She regularly couldn't fall asleep without taking sleeping pills
But once sound asleep she was back to her typical anarchist self
No attempt to respect craftsmanship
So as to make the length of the bed into the width
So as to put her pillow on the wrong side of the bed

All I saw was her photograph tucked between the pages of a
  book
Her gaze beyond the lens
Was as innocent as a village girl
Or a village woman   I should say
For there remains the fact of her failed marriage
I know the man who broke up with her
I also know that she's presently in love with Jiangnan
She expressed all her ideals in her poetry
Defying her homeland in the Peninsula
She's created a love nest on a sandbar in the river
There she kept ducks and grew vegetables
And implanted Jiangnan's seeds in her womb
And became a genuine no-nonsense village woman
And let flower-like girls blossom in her home garden

Perhaps because of her fiddling away time at home on the
Peninsula
She had come to bear a maritime personality
In Jiangnan she so adored
Hung He would gush down all the way pouring into the Eastern
Sea
As though the river would flood the peak of Mt. Taishan
She thirsted for the Hung He to flood the Peninsula and pour
  into her

She was fortunate
To greatly contribute to the South-North Water Transfer
And shrink the distance of love

Hu-hu-hu the incessant voice I hear
Covers up no small sorrow of hers
Injured in fate's surprise attack
Dressed in a tattered, wadded coat
She once demanded official justice for her father killed in a
traffic accident
She also has a yen for the Occident a little
Yearning to visit St. Petersburg and Siberia
To listen to the bells of Christian churches with spires

                                    – Translation by Kyoko Yoshida

Always   Tian Yuan
かならず   田原

Always go back among people
To listen attentively to their mockeries and insults
  and to reflect on violence
Always go out to the square
To denounce a dogma and expose a deceit

Scrutinize the altered history always
To restore its truth
Pursue and regain the lost memories always
To let them resurface

Confront the roaring ocean always directly
To sorrow over its cruelty with the ocean itself
Look up always at a hawk that revolves above
To superpose my gaze from its wings

Always learn from the mountain peak
—A sharp sword penetrating the dark clouds!
Always identify the murmurs from a hearse midair
Among the echoes in the canyon

Become always a blazing torchlight
To shine upon one person forever
Always turn into a shooting star
To glide yonder into the dark night

Always go back to the T'ang poetry
To review the wisdom of the ancients
Always look at the civilization with suspicion
Not to bring Earth toward devastation

Always imagine the Sun God of the cave mural
To unveil the past unimaginable pain beneath his smile
Always blow a clay flute when excavated
To test if it still plays the sorrow of the bygone days

Always question myself
What if I were an other
Always give the world a second look to ask
If this world is separate from that world

– Translation by Kyoko Yoshida

**Fire Spinning Festival
at Aso Shrine**
火振り神事

Jeffrey Angles
ジェフリー・アングルス

light the bundle of reeds
once it catches, spin it
on the attached rope
the flames form an arc
burning even more brightly
carried by centrifuge
flames soar and dance
but tightly tethered
its destiny is determined
always tracing the same path

centrifugal force also governs the soul
like burning reeds we move
outward from our birthplace
rocking as we run
but invisible ropes
hold us back
our flight ends
in an orbit with
a small radius

as it flies in circles
the soul burns brilliant scarlet
but it is just a dream
the rope will break
freeing us from our orbit
a vision we see again and again
meanwhile we wait emptily
until that day we suddenly
fly off in a straight line

alone in the darkness
a ball of fire
scattering sparks

Wisdom Teeth, or   Jeffrey Angles
On Not Knowing One's Parents   ジェフリー・アングルス
親知らず

I do not know the name of the woman who gave birth to me
The reason is that she is not the person
Whom I call mother
Was she short or tall?
What did she look like?
Was she blond like me?
Where did she come from?
Whom did she live with?
With whom did she share love?
Did it hurt when I was born?
Did she ask for an anesthetic?
Was she alone in the delivery room
Or was there someone to hold her hand?
When she handed me over to the hospital
Did she turn this way?
Did she see my face
Clearly?
No way to know

So when the dentist
Looked into my mouth

And told me of my ancestry
For the first time
It was not because of the anesthesia
That my mouth couldn't move
One can read the land of one's ancestors
From the angle of the wisdom teeth
The dentist told me

As I hang my heavy head
And fall into sleep
My ancestors crowd their way
Into my mind's eye, their Gaelic
Overflowing with vowels
And in the middle, there she stands
Her unknown outlines
Taking vague, indistinct form
For the first time
In the moment
My wisdom teeth
Are plucked out

Author's Note: This poem describes a true story that happened when I went to have my wisdom teeth removed. As an adoptee, I grew up wondering about my ancestry and birth mother almost constantly. The word for *wisdom tooth* in Japanese is *oya shirazu*, literally "not knowing one's parents." The reason is that wisdom teeth grow in during adolescence as one is moving away from and forgetting one's relationship to one's parents. Ironically, it was when I went to have my wisdom teeth out that I got the first hint about my birth family.

Editor's Note: Angles' poems written originally in Japanese and translated by the author.

From the Series
Learning Japanese
「日本語を学ぶこと」

Andrew Campana
アンドリュー・カンパーナ

When I speak
Japanese,
This:
   • an applauding jellyfish
   • a cloud within a cloud
   • two anxious dolphins
   • a shrieking sandbox
   • grilled meat skewers
   • a rotating fan
   • a long, narrow red carpet
   • toaster oven at 750W for 15 minutes
Is what becomes of my tongue.

∞

Typing
In Japanese
Is DIFFICU^{difficult}meaning

Typing
In Japanese
Is dreamhillstrong^{difficult}LT

Typing
In Japanese
Is nonmapmorphwill^{difficult}position

∞

41

Japanese vocabulary list
Longer than my nerves
air mail   express delivery postmark   delivery date
Are these new words
Postally circling
From brain to lips
"Delayed delivery" = *enchaku, enchaku, enchaku*
Sound of a dropped signature stamp.

∞

nihongo wo
romaji de yomu toki
sukoshi iwakan ga aru
bogo to onaji arufabetto
mitai da ga
sonnani perapera yomu no wa
uso no you ni omoeru

ウエンアイライトジャパニーズ
インローマンレッターズ
イットフィールズアビットオッド
イットルックスライク
マイネーティブアルファベット、バット
リーディングウィズサッチイーズ
フィールズライクアドリーム

When I write Japanese
In Roman letters
It feels a bit odd
It looks like
My native alphabet, but
Reading with such ease
Feels like a dream

∞

42

The secret to Japanese
Lies at the ocean floor in a box within a box within a box
Within a cat within a box within a box within a box within
A box within a box within a box within a box
Within a box within a box within a cat within
A box within a box within a mouse within a box
Within a box within a box within a box within
A cat within a box within a box within a box
Within a box within a box within a box within
A box within a box within a box within a box
Within a box within a box within a box within
A box within a box within a box within a box
Within a whale within a box within a box within
A box.
Too bad, eh?

∞

I finally arrived at Japanese
Just four hours on the Shinkansen
But walking, it's taken eight years
I looked at the gate and the roof
particle   door   particle   window   noun
My passport long since dismembered
Into pa   and ss   and port
Blown off in a gale
Foreign resident card crushed, minted into coin
The currency of this new country
I search for birds through my binoculars
Crows perched on lines of a sheet of paper
Crying out crying out crying out crying out

– Translations by Jordan A. Y. Smith

Town Square in Early Spring   **Hirokawa Chiaki**
早春の広場   廣川ちあき

The cathedral bell sounds racing round the town square
Transform into horse with pliant legs
Sunday morn at eleven o'clock
Too early to be loafing
Too late to go walking
In this square where the horse raced off to some town under
young springtime,
Leaving nothing but
The usual comings-and-goings of people
That a sky so cloudy could brim with such brilliance
I've never known
Or rather,
Just now, I've realized its certainty

– Translation by Jordan A. Y. Smith

The Freeze Returns   Hirokawa Chiaki
凍って返る   廣川ちあき

On a night when *sakura* fall in such profusion
You can't sleep with the windshield wipers down,
This I have been raised to believe

Softening the contours of every last thing
At two-degrees Celsius, drifts of petals begin to freeze,
Though the morning of pure brightness comes streaming in, all
the more
No letting go of things buried

Like cold prickling pain
Deep night forces itself so distant
Breathstoppingly so, from my body   somehow
Right straight yet warped in its path
Enfolding me   somehow
I yearn to be buried
Truly

Cars aligned properly in the lot en masse
Growing wipers slanting out like horns,
Far too sharp
For a night when *sakura* fall in such profusion

                    – Translation by Jordan A. Y. Smith

The Film Buff   **Nakauchi Komoru**
映画好き男   中内こもる

At my agency, there's this creepy young guy.
This creepy young guy likes pop idols and pro wrestling and
video games.
I am not at all saying that
  pop idols and pro wrestling and video games are creepy.
The creepy thing is: this guy.
This guy looks like an enormous mushroom.
Of course, I'm not saying mushrooms are bad.
On the contrary, I love mushrooms.
However, people who look like large mushrooms are creepy.

He's 31 years old yet has no jobs going.
But this guy loves movies and watches a ton of them.
"Have you seen *Mystic River*?" he asks me one day.
"You're supposedly an actor but you haven't even seen *Mystic
River*, that's insane. You should *totally* watch it,"
  says the enormous mushroom.

Mystic River is a mystery film produced in 2003.
Directed by Clint Eastwood.
Starring Sean Penn, Tim Robbins, and Kevin Bacon.
Kevin Bacon, one of the top three tastiest sounding names in
Hollywood, Kevin Bacon.
The other two, I'd never heard of.
Anyway, it's a famous mystery movie
  that got the Academy Award for Best Actor.

Sean Penn plays the lead role as an ex-con,
  now the owner of a corner store.
The story begins with his daughter
  having just been murdered by somebody.

Kevin Bacon is a detective
  who is also Sean Penn's childhood friend.
Kevin Bacon is the one who tells Sean Penn,
"We found your daughter's body."
"And Sean Penn's reaction is just amazing!" Mushroom rants.
Normally, if someone were told their daughter's been murdered,
they'd be like: *"Why! It can't be!"*
all ranting and raving.
However, Sean Penn at that moment just reacts like—

        "What...? What...?"

Certainly, people might react that way when suddenly faced
with extreme situations.

I've gotta see this.
My interest piqued,
So I paid the hundred yen at the rental shop and watched it,
and—
That scene was nowhere to be found.
True enough, his daughter is killed.
But Kevin Bacon never goes to tell Sean Penn the news.
While Kevin Bacon is waffling about how to break it to him,
Sean Penn finds out about it on his own.
And he says,   *"Why! It can't be!"*
He is raving all over the place.
And I found myself standing in front of the TV going—

        "What...? What...?"

The film was pretty average.

        — Translation by Andrew Campana and Jordan A.Y. Smith

Veteran   Nakauchi Komoru
ベテラン   中内こもる

Can we please have a refill of water?
My girlfriend just started chugging it down.
Elegant without any air of stuffiness:
  one of my favorite restaurants.
My girlfriend sits in front of me chugging water.
The people we're supposed to meet haven't arrived.
She just chugs another glass.
Can we please have a refill of water?
"How is that *you're* the nervous one here?"
I'm the one here to meet her parents.
So I'm the one who's supposed to be freaking out.
"I'd like to ask your blessing to marry Sayuri."
I'm the one who has to face them and get these words out.
So there's no reason for you to be sitting in front of me
  chugging away like this.
It's okay. Believe in me. After all: I'm a veteran.

Still…somehow the nervousness has spread to me.
I must admit, no matter how many times I meet the parents,
  it's always uncomfortable.
That's right.
Because even a pro soccer player,
after hundreds, thousands of times taking the field,
Will get a bit shaky if his World Cup final match goes to a
tie-breaking penalty shoot-out.
And since this is only my eleventh time,
it's a given I'm gonna get nervous.

Oh, yeah.
After we're done with the conversation, let's go shop for rings.
I know a great shop.
They're my go-to ring sellers.

What?
I'm supposed to buy one in secret and surprise you with it?
I've done it so many times, I must have gotten mixed up.
Don't worry about the finances.
It's alright—my point card is full from previous purchases.
I'm entitled to a 100,000 yen discount.

Parents running a bit late, eh?
She's drinking water again.
It's alright, I'm telling you. I've never come to a restaurant
  to have this talk and been refused.
This is an auspicious place.
Hey, next Sunday let's go, just the two of us,
  to check out our new condo.
Wait, actually, no-can-do next week.
School sports festival.
My daughter from my fourth wife has a sports festival.
Will you seriously stop chugging water?

Her parents finally arrive, and we exchange greetings.
Sayuri's father denies us his blessing to marry.
What for? Is there something wrong with me?
Is it because I'm a ten-time failure?
True enough,
I get how a man divorced ten times would inevitably
raise a few eyebrows in wonder at my fickleness.
But please just hear me out.
It wasn't my repeated flightiness that led to my admittedly
whopping number of divorces.
I sincerely loved each of those women.
It just turned out that the ultimate result was separation.
It could happen to anyone.

Is that not so?

According to her parents,
Sayuri's track record is *fifteen* divorces.

Got a point card at the same store.

You know what, just forget our whole conversation today.
I mean seriously—*fifteen times*?

— Translation by Andrew Campana and Jordan A.Y. Smith

Crab Warehouse

蟹倉庫

Oshima Takeo

大島健夫

Dawn breaks in the crab warehouse
The crabs have just finished counting heads in the break room,
  and pinching their punch cards with their pinchers
They walk sideways to their workspace
Their work is to manage the boxes of canned crab
  the warehouse is packed with
Today they start from rack number 17
The morning sun shines in from above the rack
The chilly air in the warehouse is tinted with dust
The crabs shuffle towards rack number 17
Their hourly wage consists of ten dried water fleas
If they are promoted to the A-team they get twelve
A livable wage if you don't spend it frivolously
From the break room they have a view of the sea
Where they all used to be some time ago
The crabs are working, going down, going up
From one rack to the next
All the racks are packed with cans
Every now and then there is an avalanche of cans
Whenever that happens, someone is squashed to death
Yesterday three crabs were squashed
The red-clawed crab who was great at singing was
  squashed under rack 49
The always intimate Japanese mud crab husband and wife were
  squashed under rack 22
The husband died instantaneously, but the wife was not
    squashed thoroughly enough so it took quite a while
    for her to die
Her entrails were hanging out as her pincer shivered for hours
"It's so cold," she said
"Please—cover me in tidal mud"

However no one had any mud
No mud was to be found anywhere in the warehouse
Everyone pretended not to notice and kept working
Going down, going up
From one rack to the next,
It was written on the recruitment leaflet:
This is a place where dreams come true
Not that crabs dream or anything
But if that is what is written, then maybe they do
As long as the crabs keep working, that is satisfactory
Overtime work's optional, but naturally everyone does it
Because everyone loves this work
Because of this crab warehouse everyone can get by
Until someday they are completely worn out
They keep working until they go inside this can
Thankful for everything they keep working
Dawn breaks in the crab warehouse
The crabs have just finished counting heads in the break room,
  and they walk sideways to the assembly line
The morning sun shines upon the racks
The squashed crabs of yesterday were cleaned up in the night
  and sent to the crab factory
Soon they'll be turned into canned crab and brought here
The crabs face the light waving their pincers,
Here we go, another day on the job
Just another day on the job

– Translation by Jonas Engesvik

Do You Remember the Skull?

頭蓋骨を覚えていますか

Oshima Takeo

大島健夫

Do you remember the
Skull?
Do you remember that big
Skull?
Do you remember that big, white skull
Above the water fountain in the park, impaled on a silver pole?

Did you ever stop to ask
Whose skull it was?
Do you know
If the skull was real or not?
You really loved it, that skull
Well then, I'll be waiting under the skull
You always used to tell me
No matter where we were going or what we were doing
It began from under that skull.

Under that skull
Together, when we shared our first kiss
The wind was blowing, the skull clattering
Clattering, clattering
Do you remember
The gentle sounds it made?
You told me then
I don't want to go anywhere anymore
And I felt the same, I wanted to be there always
Under that skull, together with you always.

Last night, I dreamt of you
We were under that parks'
Skull

Without saying anything we gazed into each other's eyes
I wanted to ask you
Am I living life to the fullest or not?
Am I working hard to become happier, or not?

Do you remember the
Skull?
That skull where you always used to wait for me
Above the water fountain in the park, impaled on a silver pole
That big, white skull.
Last night, I dreamt of you
We were together under that skull
Gazing deeply into each other's eyes.

                              – Translation by Jonas Engesvik

Lost Items   **Ishiwata Kimi**
なくしもの   石渡紀美

My child lost a shoe
I was carrying him, yet didn't even notice
Just one
In a blink, slipped off   gone forever

Why is it that, when something gets lost,
It's the parents, rather than the child, who get flustered to the
                    point of tears

Kids don't care
Whether they find themselves half shoeless
Whether the bag stuffed in raincoat pocket disappears
They forget in a blink   to be absorbed again in play
Parents, alone, dwell eternally on these lost items,
Though in truth, with such things,
They'd do as well to shrug it off like molting skin,
Like that long lost fragment of their own youth, one could say

Children leave parents behind to zoom ahead,
Even as parents are pressing the bell at the Lost and Found

– Translation by Jordan A. Y. Smith

Mother's House   Ishiwata Kimi
母の家   石渡紀美

Fallen in the center of the living room,
Miscellany had lain scattered through the room
But now arranged back into usual spots,
Old newspapers bundled
The pack of remote controls in appropriate den

Straightening up a house gone motherless,
Closing up all the doors and drawer
Left open like the mouth of my sleeping mother,
Rice steamer cabinet door
Cutlery drawer
Dish tower drawer
Closet door
TV stand door
Dresser drawers
Mother's existence was bound to open doors and drawers

Upon finishing the clean-up consisting of simply closing the
               open doors and drawers,
Mother's house seemed to accept the absence of its master
But for me, her daughter, that will take a bit more time.

– Translation by Jordan A. Y. Smith

My Big Baby, Earth   **Fuzuki Yumi**
大きく産んであげるね、地球   文月悠光

When I close my eyes, I disappear.
In a blink interval,
In that lone moment of blackness,
My body becomes another something.
My getting pregnant with the Earth
Was not through anyone's trickery.
Unfurling a one-act cosmos across the inside of my eyelids,
From here on out, I will remember.

If you're going to treat me like a kid,
Earth, I'm gonna give birth to *you*—kid.
Inflate you inside my uterus,
Surreptitiously rotate you.
Your fledgling axis-spin skills at times causing
You to awkwardly bump up against my uterine walls.
With your premature gravitation
Incessantly spilling sand all over the cosmos.
Its dry rustling,
Like the sounds of scrawled characters,
Announcing my pregnancy.

Time to prepare for this Earth pregnancy. First, to tread the
downy shadows of baby hair, to knead away in the mud.
Pointing fingers at each bit that emits smoke, indicating them
one by one,
   (I do this to you)
each time I pry open my clenched eyes, I see myself therein, so
want to torment you all the more.
In order to pour the seas all over you, time and again I shove you.
When this has softened your edges thoroughly—try giving
yourself a spin. You're spinning way better, I bet.

I'll birth you way bigger than the others, Earth
    I brag.
I rub my belly crosswise, pat my sides and sigh.
Floating in space, I'll know your blue for the first time.
If there's nowhere for me to stand,
First I'll give birth.
(Can you forgive me?)
Standing right atop her babe, one of *those* moms.
Once again today, you've grown
Far too tall.

– Translation by Jordan A. Y. Smith

A Snow of Bone   Fuzuki Yumi
骨の雪   文月悠光

On back of a black funeral dress
Comes fluttering down to form drifts:
Bone powder.
Chopsticks clutched in hand, I glance down:
The shoulder of my uniform is also white.
Grandfather's ashes cross the chopstick like a bridge.
The one my uncle just reached for,
Unmistakably, was his knee bone.
> (Grandfather's knee, always warm. Seeking its warmth, I
> ventured into his vegetable garden. Rustling sounds of
> potatoes swelling underground. Cornstalks bore aloft golden
> crowns. From leafy shadows peeked the deep green of
> *kabocha* pumpkins. My grandfather's shadow floated over

them, and I gazed up to the sky. As I did, something touched
my forehead. White flakes came to blanket the garden soil.
The drifting snow clothed my limbs. Morning of the year's
first snow dawned in grandfather's garden.)
The bone is passed my way—I gulp down a breath.
My chopsticks sink in surprisingly deep.
A dazzle of powder billows.
Seated in her wheelchair, my grandmother
Stared at the fine snow.
Even without you here, we have to go on living.
Faces feigning ignorance, we have to go on living.
Inside the urn,
Newly incinerated hot bones
Mutter something or other.
All of us, weep.

Grandmother reaches her chopsticks toward the Adam's apple.
Two trembling sticks pinch the small, round throat bone.
New breath whirls into the billows,
As I clasp my hands together.
Through laughter and loss alike,
We here on this side
Go on living,
Leaving a snow of bone to pile up.

– Translation by Jordan A. Y. Smith

Memory of Summer　　　　　　　　　　　**Tanaka Atsusuke**
夏の思い出　　　　　　　　　　　　　　　田中宏輔

summer
white summer
memory of summer
reflections of light
concrete
clubs
locker rooms
you were on the volleyball team
you shone
dazzling to the eyes
me lined up
sitting down
I was on the judo team
we were still freshmen
summer
white summer
memory of summer
reflections of light
overlapping
hands and
hands and
sweat and
light
white light
reflecting
concrete
dark shadows
no one was there
that day
that summer
that summer vacation

that time
was just our time
just you and me
you and me
(just you and me, right?)
you shone
summer
white summer
sun
that day
was my first time
I didn't know
that it was such a ticklish place
the lips
touching scanty whiskers
(just a few, no matter how you let them grow, right?)
lips and
sweat and
dazzling
it lasted
only
a moment
summer
a memory
of white summer
a first kiss
(you did taste of sweat, didn't you?)
but
that was all
that was all
that day
that time
that time anyone ever saw you
we didn't stay at the camp
the teams ended early

why
did you go
out for a swim
with her
in the sea?
summer
a summer
day
white memory of summer
forever shining
my
your
summer
day
the memory of that summer day
flipping through summers
flipping through
each time I come to it
it tears my heart
apart
tears my heart
to shreds
then scatters them
to the wind
summer
white summer
memory of summer
reflected light
concrete
clubs
locker rooms
overlapping
hands and
eyes and
lips and

sweat and
light and
shadow and
summer

— Translation by Jeffrey Angles

Under the Umbrella   Tanaka Atsusuke
カサのなか   田中宏輔

under the umbrella
I hear your voice clearly

the rain filters away
everything unnecessary

all that reaches my ears
is the sound of your voice

— Translation by Jeffrey Angles

Burying the Sun   Tanaka Atsusuke
陽の埋葬   田中宏輔

A moonlit shore,
An angel with folded wings leaned his ear toward the voice of
the waves.

A moonlit shore,
An angel leaned in with his lost ear to listen to the voice of the
waves.

A moonlit shore,
The voice of the waves whispered to the angel the whereabouts
of his lost ear.

A moonlit shore,
The angel murmured he needed the ear no more.

                                  — Translation by Jeffrey Angles

Selected Tanka:
Noguchi Ayako 野口あや子

Translations by Nihei Chikako and Andrew Houwen

苺ジャム、こんなにおいしいものはない　あなたの髪に塗ってあげたい

there's nothing
more delicious than
strawberry jam –
I want to run it
through your hair

耳を閉じたり耳をあけたりするように酸いも甘いも食べたいものを

like covering
and uncovering
your ears –
bitter or sweet
eat what you want

撫でられて咲く耳だからそよ風のままのピアノがいちばん好きよ

soothing
my ears, making
them bloom
piano music in the breeze
is what they like most of all

「休憩中」に似合う絵文字を考えて考えていて休憩おわる

thinking
and thinking about
the right emoji
for 'on my break' –
break time's over

リトルブラックボイ　世紀の発明はときに女性を狂わせたり

little black boy –
the inventions
of the centuries
have at times
made women mad

終電を知らせてあげる羊、羊、ひつじたち数えあっておやすみ

announcing
the last train –
sheep
sheep sheep
good night

Selected Haiku:
Suzuno Umine 涼野海音

Translations by Nihei Chikako and Andrew Houwen

倉庫から転がるボール蝶の昼

ball rolling
out of the shed –
midday butterfly

マラソンの一列鳥の巣の下を

a line
of marathon runners
under a bird's nest

行く人も来る人もなき春野かな

nobody coming
or going –
spring field

短夜やロシア映画に大き森

summer night –
in a Russian film
a vast forest

ボート漕ぐ後ろに森の暗さあり

rowing a boat –
behind, the forest's
darkness

青大将テニスコートをよぎりをり

crossing over
the tennis court –
a rat snake

誰もゐぬベッドの上の蛍籠

nobody there –
above the bed
a cage of fireflies

泣きやまぬ赤子八月十五日

a newborn baby
that won't stop crying –
August the fifteenth[1]

---

[1] This refers to the dropping of the atomic bombs and Japan's surrender in 1945.

草矢打つ明石の海のまぶしさに

the sea at Akashi –
shooting grass arrows
in its dazzling light[2]

新神戸駅で降りたる捕虫網

getting off
at Shin Kōbe Station –
rockpooling net

芋虫の背にひとすぢのひかりかな

along the back
of the caterpillar –
a thread of light

自転車の二つ並んで天の川

two bicycles
lined up side by side –
the Milky Way

---

[2] 'Shooting grass arrows' refers to a child's game, in which grass or reeds are made into an arrow's shape. Akashi is a city on the Seto Inland Sea, at the western edge of Kōbe.

東京の地図に雨つぶ星祭

on a Tokyo map
a speck of rain –
star festival[3]

機関庫の奥に日の差す十二月

reaching to the back
of the locomotive shed –
December sunlight

予備校の窓灯りゐるクリスマス

the lights still on
in the cram school –
Christmas

サボテンの花赤々と寝正月

the bright red
of the cactus flowers –
New Year's at home

---

[3] The Star Festival, or Tanabata, celebrates the meeting of the deities Orihime and Hikoboshi (represented by the stars Vega and Altair), and is held on the seventh day of the seventh month of the lunar calendar. The lovers are separated by the Milky Way and can only meet once a year, on this day.

Heaven and Earth
大崎清夏

I hear a song as I step in
I look but no one is singing
Crows cool themselves under roof of the fountain
Dogs compete to show their breeding
Comfort lodges in the profiles of the people

Why is someone here who isn't?
I wonder if I'm just mistaken
I wonder if this slight misfortune
Might take form and show itself

The song seems to sing
Of some happening in the distant past
That became part of people, made them weep
Then was forgotten completely

The song comes from the water's edge
I hear it not in my ears
But in my backbone

– Translation by Jeffrey Angles

Ōsaki Sayaka
大崎清夏

71

Pointing Impossible   Ōsaki Sayaka
指差すことができない   大崎清夏

The conference to determine boundaries
Is once again being held everywhere today
Health has lost its definition
It hurts to absorb
It hurts to excrete
So the only other choice
Is to have fun at work
The girls were smiling
As they pulled the seaweed
Growing like black hair on the rough rocks
And ate it
And sold it
Getting sick is a happy thing
Seeing the color of blood is a happy thing
Among the muddy twilight flow and bundle of knives
They work on their feet, jumping about on white legs
A record of the wind and earth, a study in customs
Someone's regular heartbeat grows irregular
And you raise the thumb of your right hand
Please come again tomorrow
I want to hear your voice so please come
Please tell me a story
It's hard being on my own
Not working
Not married
Not fighting to the death
Through a combination of vague maternal instinct
And a forgetful instinct to flee
I was always idling my time away
I'm covered in wrinkles
But look at the texture of my skin
Look how small my pores are

That's right
I'm proud
That is the new definition of health
Among the girls of this island
They have fun as they work
The prohibitions have finally been lifted
The aroma of a kerosene heater
I drink a little beer
But the cheese is for the young ones
I like it too
Ha-ha-ha, tee-hee-hee-hee-hee
Those migrant birds with the yellow beak
Have they been eradicated or not?
No one seems to know
Maybe they're just hiding
Like a sea urchin out of reach of the diver's hand
It's been sixty years since I came here as a newlywed
There's been misfortune, fate, and happiness
No one gets to choose
She's also my friend
Everyone here are friends
When I pray to the god of the sea
I can see his face clearly
His face is made up of waves and bubbles
So it's impossible to point it out
The blood under your textured skin
Does not flow in streaks
Like fibrous little roots
Like the sound of a gamelan
It seeps into twilight on the rocky shore

                          – Translation by Jeffrey Angles

The Terrorists   Ōsaki Sayaka
テロリストたち   大崎清夏

The room is quiet
There is no door, only a window
That is how everyone gets in
That is how everyone gets out
The window is large
The window is quiet
The window is filled with the sea of grass beyond

When night falls
A sleepless couple sneaks in
Placing their wet hands on the windowsill
(The couple are stark naked)
(Intruders are welcome)
(Owners are turned away)
They are not Adam and Eve
The couple rarely bathe
And smell slightly greasy
Perhaps they are penniless
But the room doesn't care
(Intruders are clean)
(They are naked after all)
The room is restful in its emptiness
Look out the window through which you entered
Surely you'll feel a beautiful thrill

The view is good from the room
Of the distant towns where they never lived
Of the distant stars which crowd the night sky
Of the wild, spiraling eyes of a wolf couple
Of the entire field of grass

The room was full of longing
It yearned for the naked couple
It yearned to leave and go somewhere
The room felt it
(Walls on three sides, that is too many)
(A window on one side, that is too few)
The room was too protected
(Goodness, even the nails were pounded in too far)
The greasy, naked couple
Will have such an easy time leaving
With one leg astride the windowsill
They'll throw themselves easily into the wind

The room doesn't yet despair
It should be possible to leave
There is a big window after all

The window is big
The window is quiet

– Translation by Jeffrey Angles

The Sorceress' Triumph
魔女の勝利

Yosuke Tanaka
田中庸介

It's not that a couple will necessarily divorce just because they don't love each other any longer. They examine the menu of fried shrimp, pork or chicken or minced-meat cutlets. Umbrellas move through the rain. Don't know if she'll cut it with everyday sensitivities. The sorceress sings a hymn. A fox tries to lure her into the forest but she won't go. She's like a houseplant now. Her pager goes off. This kind of thing almost never happens in rainy London. She wets her umbrella again running to make the call. Yes, it turned out successful, diagram-like, just as planned. Congratulations! the boss said. Thank you. Lay down, or the time bomb will go off again. Look at the beauty of those roof tiles shattering, and the bananas. To the man in the street it must appear to be a flash of lightning at dawn. The squeezing of lemons. The fruit dying as it is squeezed. Fallen leaves piled and rotting on walkways of a solitary island. Bugs hatching. It's the sorceress' teatime.

The sorceress jogs alone in the park every morning. She runs too much and has injured her knees. This brings an end to her happy everyday life. Trying to overtake a woman in a culvert who looked her way and said, look, farmed fish are nasty! Watch, they are about to escape the net. The catfish that feel a moment's freedom are again captured in the afternoon. That, say the people who know, is the history of this country. She's going to the hospital. The TV is overdoing a show featuring a bitter song and dance done by the last agricultural tribe. The song gets an exaggeratedly good rating and wins an award. The prize money slipped into a silent hand, is handsome. She's so lonely that she's watching the moon tonight. Don't grumble so much all the time! She uses body shampoo in the outdoor hotsprings bath. Suds build and fill the space to overflowing. Her knee still hurts.

Just what if thunder peeled here, what would happen? We'd have to cover our bellybuttons. The sorceress having slathered herself with lotion all over slips and falls in the bath. Wakame seaweed hangs to dry. She hides in the opaque bathwater. Shoot! She disappears. Shoot! The stage goes dark. It is not knowledge that was intentionally extinguished before. When the hallway went dark the lights came on. In the middle of all this some good can come.

Yes, they scatter. The cherry blossoms that bloom must scatter their petals, and it becomes the season of the leaves. She wants a ruby ring! Was the timetable checked? Is service important? An urgent telegraph is sent stating that the sorceress was discovered. I am tired of all this! They said her whereabouts were unknown. He takes the Yokosuka Line to work. Did you get the power on? Well, at least that is taken care of. Let's have a simple meal of bread and milk. Why don't we celebrate our success with Champagne? To human happiness! The sorceress goes to driver's training. There was an anonymous report of her being seen eating curry rice with someone and talking all friendly and happy in the springtime. When going home drunk it started to snow. Let's have a snowball fight. I'll kill you.

I dye my hair blond. We form a band and scream. We wear masks. Look! Wave! Squeeze me. Listen you can hear a violin. It suits you that depressingly sweet smell of a protein drink. No need for you to put on a play with some depraved story. Ah, the sorceress is about to cross Dai-Bosatsu Peak. The sweet and wet smell of a white magnolia in the rain. On the mountain a single giant magnolia tree is in bloom. A stillness arises. Lights shine on the flowers. This is the best of times.

The mountain of salt will explode. Everything will explode. I disagree. I like the snowfall of cherry blossom petals, a bout of palsy and flying off to Mt. Fuji, the psychedelic spring nonsense of hallucinating green fireflies. A high voltage insulator waiting at a small shop that can be blown away by the wind. Pure energy accumulates. An emergency vehicle explodes the night time cherry trees on the riverbank. The crowded bus stop is completely red. An old man holding a bottle of shochu winks at the sorceress, of course she ignores him. A glittering advertisement for a criminal offense. What do you think? I am filled with doubts. You can't go home. She plays ignorant. Concern. Should I stay or should I go? Winning is losing. What? Try saying that once again. The sorceress screams on the shore of the cobalt colored sea. The sorceress' base but profound sensitivity is powerful. Get down! Looks like it's going to explode! Stop. Stop the boss up the hill with walkie-talkie commands. Look! The enemy is running this way, isn't he? We won. It's our victory. A great victory! It's ours! We did it! All out victory for us! At that moment the volcano erupted. Pillars of fire rise high into the sky. Everything turns ashen. Only the sorceress has triumphed. She dances.

– Translation by Jeffrey Johnson and Kubo Mitsuhiko

Poetry on Every Platform in 2010s Japan

by Andrew Campana

I first heard **Miya Matsuoka**'s poetry on a summer trip to Tokyo three years ago. Browsing the shelves of TACO ché—the shop on the third floor of Nakano Broadway packed to the gills with alternative zines, poetry collections, art books, comics, prints, music, and t-shirts—her album, *Limited Express 383*, caught my eye. How could it not? Posing on the cover in a smart uniform with white gloves, and surrounded by a cartoony frame with galaxies swimming behind her, Matsuoka immediately draws you into her world. I was blown away by the poems she reads on this CD, set to her own musical accompaniment; a self-proclaimed "station attendant fetishist," her intensely surreal and cerebral take on the vast universe of Tokyo's public transportation was like nothing I had heard before. The two poems selected here give a taste both of the themes that preoccupy her and her unique approach towards them: she crafts kaleidoscopic reveries from everyday commutes, transmuting them into scenes that rapidly shift from the whimsical to the visceral and then back again.

From her Twitter feed—I had just realized that Twitter was the platform of choice for Japan's contemporary poetry scene—I learned about the annual event, Poeket, happening the very next day. Poeket is a convention where poets from Tokyo and beyond gather to sell their own handmade and small press collections, anthologies, CDs, and zines. It was there that the enormous diversity of contemporary poetry in Tokyo finally sank in—poets of all ages, backgrounds, and genders writing and performing works on every topic and in every form imaginable and unimaginable were represented there. Along with Matsuoka's work, I aim to give *ToPoJo*'s readers just a small taste in translation of some of the most brilliant figures I've come across at innumerable readings, open mics, talk shows, lectures, workshops, and exhibits in the city, since then.

Ayaka Satō is certainly one of these extraordinary poets, taking the compact traditional form of the haiku with its strict syllabic counts and required nods to seasonality, and making them into something utterly fresh and contemporary, while still retaining a sense of mystery and wonder. At one point she compares the sight of newly-green trees in the late spring to "the sharp water of eyedrops," and each of her haiku have a similar intensity of vision, crossing classical tropes of flowers, animals, and natural settings with the detritus of the 2010s and making sparks fly every time.

One thing that draws together many of the young poets working in Japan today is their use of digital technologies—not just the aforementioned Twitter, but actively using computers and the internet to continually think up new ways to share their work, and to compose new kinds of poems that cannot help but be profoundly influenced by current media environments. Satoko Kono and Ryōta Yamada are two members of the "verbal art unit" TOLTA, a furiously creative quartet that keeps all of Kanto on its toes with their innovative poetry performances, workshops, and exhibitions.

One of **Satoko Kono**'s most recent collections is entitled *WWW/Panda Chant*, and was distributed mainly through digital channels like Kindle; she is also an avid blogger, and the poem translated here appeared on her blog before it did in her most recent collection, as is frequently the case in recent years. In a way very much in line with her vast knowledge and appreciation of avant-garde movements throughout history—evidenced by her recent TOLTA poetry events in honour of the 100th anniversary of Dada—"Fortune Teller" evokes Futurist and Surrealist works, both poetry and painting. Abstract elements and entities collide with nature that is not quite nature, machines that are not quite machines, and characters and voices that seem to approach but not arrive at being human.

Ryōta Yamada's award-winning collection from last year, *Obama Google*, is a masterwork of conceptual poetry. These are poems that emerge directly not just from contemporary digital media, but from the modes of reading, writing, consumption, and attention that these platforms encourage (or coerce)—from the titular Google search suggestions related to the previous U.S. President, to "Wikipedia Parade" translated here, a stunning recreation of the all-too-familiar sensation of falling down a Wikipedia rabbit hole clicking link after link after link.

Kazuhiro Yada's most recent poetry collection, *Hyōka, Raigai: RPG Poetics*, is named after two characters from an obscure, free online role-playing game called "Histore." Drawing from pop culture and forms of new media storytelling for inspiration, his poems constantly shift in tone and form, and are replete with references to mysterious places and figures—whether he is alluding to the game world or his own inner world, is unclear. The poems excerpted here from this much longer work show just a glimpse of the diversity of his technique, moving from stanzas filled with arcane language, to video game walkthrough-style diction, to manifesto mode, to smartphone automatic text suggestion-based text generation, to stream of consciousness. As with Kono, this book was self-published online and is available in Japan's Kindle store, complete with a stunning, kaleidoscope-like cover.

Its cover was designed by perhaps one of the most innovative figures in the global poetry scene today, the Tokyo poet and artist **ni_ka**, a translation of whose "Record of Affidavit" is included here. This poem is remarkable within ni_ka's output not only for being her first and only poem in print, but the only one of her works that could even be reproduced on paper media. The rest of her oeuvre lives in cyberspace, or at least those places where the "virtual" touches "our world." Like concrete poetry for a new era, her "monitor" poems are composed for the screen and make dramatic use of colours, animations, emoji, and special effects, and have to be read through dense clouds of flowers, sparkles, hearts, raindrops, and stars that continuously explode across the page; her "AR [Augmented Reality] Poems" must be "read" through special smartphone apps that make similar flurries of words and images appear to manifest in the "real" world through the phone camera, most poignantly used in a project exploring new ways of mourning after the Tōhoku triple disaster in March 2011. The poem translated here brings us full circle—that circle being the Yamanote Line, perhaps—back to Matsuoka, with a dreamlike poetic center inspired by Tokyo's public transportation, nestled in a collage-like legal form from an alternate universe with no two sections sharing the same font or poetic style.

What we have here, then, is poetry on every platform: subway platform, train platform, Kindle store, blog, CD, wiki, Twitter, RPG, card game, handmade zine, and on, and on. It is this relentless search for new venues, channels, and experiences of reading that to me makes these some of the most exciting works of poetry today, whether inside or outside of Japan.

Railroad Crossing   **Matsuoka Miya**
踏切   松岡宮

I wonder   where it goes
Just seven stops from the beginning to the end
At Shimo-Maruko station on the Tokyu Tamagawa line
A school of black-suited fish passes through
The railroad crossing
Bathing in the slaps of sunshine
Scrambling to get ahead, climbing and climbing and cutting
through the water
Glittering dolphin-kick ripples
A single black road was built
Through the little Shimo-Maruko shopping district
I wonder   where it goes
The scheduled departure time is already 30 seconds past
Ding   ding   ding
Me, I've never hurt a fly
On the arm of the train driver who can't sound the horn
Summer droplets trickle down in a single stream

– Translation by Andrew Campana

Round Trip   Matsuoka Miya
往復   松岡宮

Those shifts with round trip after round trip on the Tokyu
Ikegami Line—
They look like the diagram of a large intestine
Damn—I hadn't noticed
Does that mean the 7000 series trains are just bits of food?
They carry so many drunk people
That the rails shriek out desperate New Year's greetings
To make things worse
I have to be in charge of cooking today
The driver brakes by aligning both arms
The driver accelerates by aligning both arms
Snow falls—sky scrapings
Snow falls—grated daikon radishes
Oh yeah, today is chicken meatball hotpot, isn't it
The driver raises a canna lily in each hand
A fragrance spilled over from the hotpot lid
Now arriving at the terminus
Yukigaya-Ōtsuka Station

                              – Translation by Andrew Campana

Selected Haiku from "There Are Eyes in You—Wide-Open"

Satō Ayaka
佐藤文香

君に目があり見開かれ

yuzu flowers   there are eyes in you   wide-open

heading off   to sumaura   the scent of french fries

first love   seabream scales   in ice

gold dust   in snail shells   graduation

a pole   piercing through stars   merry-go-round

the sharp water   of eyedrops   the evening's newly green trees

like a snowy day   the morning sun   on the hydrangeas

the hydrangeas   in their calyces   are words

an atmosphere   garbage floating   across the setting sun

seeing a peacock   summer fruits   murmur to the forest

you play   with the night   as if it were water

a walking bird   in this world   there are joys

an unfamiliar town   in a blizzard   becomes familiar

– Translation by Andrew Campana

Fortune Teller
占い師

Kōno Satoko
河野聡子

There is no water, but there is wind, coiling into spirals, and the ship will go right through the vortices of wind, sailing just as prophesized, and far away there stands a man with a blue hat holding a flag, and there is no water but there are waves, sparks scattering every time they come into contact with the ships, and time makes sparks fly, and as soon as you touch a vortex it will disappear, don't worry, you are all safe, you are all this nation itself, the ship too, you, yourself, you can be steady and maintain this, why are you all—

Because there is—

Something like rain is falling
It's falling
It's not made to fall
There's no one making it fall,
An unexpected

Explosion.
The sound of massive light being crushed,
of living pipes tightening,
The sound
of air wrung out from those slender places
and strangled out in reverse,
then becoming silent.

Not a single ghost is speaking
A long
long
silence.

– Translation by Andrew Campana

Contemporary Poetry Wikipedia Parade

現代詩ウィキペディアパレード

Yamada Ryōta

山田亮太

starting from a reconsideration of **modern poetry**'s formalization, aestheticization, and so on, at the beginning of the **20th century** there emerged Contemporary Poetry■in traditional **form poetry** in literary language, modern people could not freely express their feelings and intentions, and used everyday language Modern Poetry■there are restrictions beyond forms like the **tanka, haiku, sonnet,** or **lüshi** Form Poetry■influenced by **phenomenology** and **existentialism** Contemporary Poetry■a method of approaching **entities** not bound to any **preconceptions** or **metaphysical** judgements Phenomenology■bringing the existence of the "existence" of "entities" into the light, the hermeneutical method Phenomenology■through the form of the possibility of understanding unintelligible words and circumstances, expression or transmission Hermeneutics■living "my" life, dying "my" **death**—one cannot escape Existentialism■in the West, founded by William Yeats, **T.S. Eliot** and others Contemporary Poetry■the world devastated after World War I, an omen of salvation T.S. Eliot■in Japan after **World War II**, a flourishing of Contemporary Poetry■the gathering of poets centred around **Nobuo Ayukawa** and **Ryūichi Tamura**'s poetry journal "**Wasteland**," well-known figures like **Shuntarō Tanikawa, Minoru Yoshioka, Amazawa Taijirō** Contemporary Poetry■joined the company but left after not coming in to work for even a day Ryūichi Tamura■"A gentleman, who was capable, but didn't really work" Ryūichi Tamura■died from esophageal cancer Ryūichi Tamura■died after collapsing from a **cerebral hemorrhage** in the middle of playing **Super Mario Bros.** with his nephew's family Nobuo Ayukawa■instead of the conventional video games fixed within a one screen display, the "side scrolling action" genre became popularized and established Super Mario Bros.■he also did many translations of mystery novels by authors such as **Agatha Christie** Ryūichi Tamura■reason she came to start writing poetry and novels, in bed with **influenza**, without any books to read Agatha Christie■was published as an **amateur literary journal** from September **1947** to June **1948** Wasteland (Poetry Journal)■in terms of methods of low-cost small-scale print runs, it used to be the case that mimeographs were almost the only way Amateur Magazines■the formation of "**The Young Japan Group**" Shuntarō Tanikawa■ an organization changed without any leadership or plan The Young Japan Group■a member of the Japan Visual Copyright Association Shuntarō Tanikawa■currently there are not many of his Japanese language teaching materials on the market Shuntarō Tanikawa■altogether 284 poems and about 150 bound works Minoru Yoshioka■A Quiet House (Shichōsha, 1968)/Poems of a Mysterious Age (Yukawa Shobō, 1974, **Shoshi Yamada** 1976)/Saffron Picking (**Seidosha**, 1978) Minoru Yoshioka■Yamada's poetry collections have a shine to them that can be distinguished at a glance on bookstore shelves Shoshi Yamada■ "Eureka"—it has been said that humanities researchers long to be published in this magazine Seidosha■Japanese **poet, French literature scholar, children's book** author, **translator.** Researcher of **Kenji Miyazawa** Amazawa Taijirō■keen on rock-collecting, called "Mr. Rocky Expert" or "Mr. Rock Expert" by his family Kenji Miyazawa■nicknamed "HELP" Kenji Miyazawa■nickname of "God" Kenji Miyazawa■common things with limited "dispersiveness" Contemporary Poetry■a work that thoroughly digests one's private viewpoint Contemporary Poetry■everyday language is already thumbed-through Contemporary Poetry■having no choice but to rely on strange linguistic expression and metaphors Contemporary Poetry■that metaphor is also thumbed-through Contemporary Poetry■seeking even more novel expressions Contemporary Poetry■esoteric and radical Contemporary Poetry■see the height of the "nonsense poetry" trend of those such as **Shōichi Nejime** and Shuntarō Tanikawa Contemporary Poetry■runs a folk art store called "Nejime Craft Shop" in **Asagaya**'s Pearl Shopping District Shōichi Nejime■enthusiastic **Shigeo Nagashima** and **Giants** fan Shōichi Nejime■a gimmick of his helmet flying off when he missed Shigeo Nagashima■bizarre and self-righteous "poetic state" Contemporary Poetry■Nagashima language/Nagashima dialect, and Japanese pseudo-Anglicisms impossible for the average person to understand Shigeo Nagashima■privacy, unintelligibility Contemporary Poetry■fan service like not knowing how far to aim Shigeo Nagashima■isolated and tapered off Contemporary Poetry■heavy and mixed use of **loanwords** Shigeo Nagashima■heavy use of interjections, modifiers, and **conjunctions** such as "well," "yeah," "so-called," "just one," "sort of" Shigeo Nagashima■double-layered expressions that developed the transformation of words that expressed the same meaning Shigeo Nagashima■the destination Contemporary Poetry■was practicing dropping his helmet while swinging his bat Shigeo Nagashima■it is before daybreak Contemporary Poetry

Note: This poem consists of quotations from the Japanese edition of Wikipedia, the free encyclopedia (accessed August 4, 2009). Phrases in subscript are the names of the cited articles; bolded phrases refer to links to those items.

– Translation by Andrew Campana

Hyōka, Raigai: RPG Poetics
ヒョウカ、ライガイ： RPG の詩学
(Excerpts)

Kazuhiro Yada
矢田和啓

#1

A purple hail is falling
People call it a super cell
Terrified   thunder still gently
Caresses you

Spring breezes carry
Applied meteorology   making volcanoes erupt
We must lower the temperature of the earth
Do the cities still not care?

Going down the slope
Like fragments of crushed words
Dazzlingly scattering
Like it were possible
For other people to inherit our lives   I wish you all happiness

Only law violations
Bind us together, only pixels
Keep us held tight
At the faculty meeting they'll be discussing me
A faculty meeting of clouds

The cloud professors hoard thunder among themselves
The cloud professors store hail among themselves

16

At the bottom of the Palace of 10,000 Demons: Hyōka.
Also at the bottom of the Palace of 10,000 Demons: Raigai.
Histoire.
This is a mystery to be unraveled.
But it has already been unraveled.
It has been unraveled that the fact that it is being unraveled has
been unraveled.
Hint.
A continuing path.

29

linked in the sky, hands
reaching out, hands
linked with hands, hands
and hands splitting open.
clouds split apart, a pair
of butterflies fly out
from the rift, breaking
through the rain and pup-
ating, that joy thrown forth.
that shout!

38

I am the Tenryū River
I am a virus
I am a minefield
I am butter
I am an eruption of smoke
I am an elementary particle
I am a myth

♭25

Architectures   of   echoes   and   light—constructions   of
reverberation and reflection

♭22

The computer is writing this poem. The computer composes a LINE message. As if to say, as if to say, as if to say, "Thank you for calling" "Thank you for coming with me today", over and over, so much that I don't know whether it's repeating it, eating it, puking it up, as if to say,

♯♭0

Your responsibilities began when you were stabbed by a spear of colorless light. Your mouth is filled with colorless light, even your ears overflow with it. This poem will probably be called Face Book. Why, why does it exist, because of Chaos, and you, you talked about a dream you had about putting dishes in the washing machine, and I, I responded with a dream I had this morning, it was a dream where I met Hirakawa-san, and I wanted to say your interpretation was wrong, but without saying anything, I woke up, and there was some Inaba Thai chicken curry left over, and I tidied up the dishes, and left the room.

– Translation by Andrew Campana

Record of Affidavit
Legal Domicile　　　*Tokyo*　SOON→
Address　**world**
(Phone number:　**9**　)
Occupation　Self-proclaimed poet Self-proclaimed artist
(Phone number:　　　）
Full Name　ni_ka
Date of Birth (DD/MM/YYYY): NO/TH/ING
To all the poetic nobodies
Even today the Yamanote Line and all of its trains go around the castle where the Emperor lives.
A yellow-green ring, going around, and around.
If this Yamanote Line track is the circumference of the belly button of Tokyo, Japan, then I am running through Tokyo,

and I get the feeling that there can be a life outside of
walking through Tokyo's brain tissue,

and I think this, every two weeks, without fail, and
then everything is taken from me, and I become
not a girl, but a beauty in men's clothing,

and I decide to draw a circle, to draw my destiny,
around and around the Yamanote line.

While dressed as a man, that is.

While supporting and supporting my inner-facing side, something that
is supposed to be right in the middle is *not there*,

so naturally, I, a girl made of nothing but vague and uncertain outlines, my
body is hardened into its masculine exterior,

in other words, the imitation called "me" takes shape through
an exterior gaze. What does this mean.

**Such a record of affidavit was
written up in this city of Tokyo.**

The Office of Contemporary Vision

– Translation by Andrew Campana

Bone Gathering   **Hachikai Mimi**
骨拾い   蜂飼耳

Why he volunteered,
Even seventy years later he couldn't say,
His reason for
Volunteering for the suicide attack squad
Only decades later, even to himself
Unknown, subtly,
Had changed footing.

Realizing this, parent and child each explored
The dark hole
With their own flashlights,
Shedding light while revealing nothing.

The child born him at age fifty
From the shadows of the bald man's prolonged death,
Raised on siphoned off nutrition,
At this point
Merely scrawls
Unsheltered characters,
As one does,
Desperate to outrun to the calendar of emotions.

One day,

They wheeled out a pushcart, on it
Placing father's bones, as yet hot,
Nothing but thighbones,
Oddly stout,
Though lying in repose
Seemingly still planted firm.

They won't fit

The employee on duty grows impatient,
On the lid, of the urn,
Presses down, hard.

Bones begin to groan,
Flustered employee's explanatory
Voice grows louder,
You're masking the uproar
Of cracking bones   fall silent.

Eventually the horizon cools,
Reveals a row of people standing in the distance
All absentminded, mouths gaping,
As though drifting into sleep, the world's heat recedes
From depths of face comes another face, gaping absently.

– Translation by Jordan A. Y. Smith

The Deer Girl   Hachikai Mimi
鹿の女   蜂飼耳

Downwind, body hidden awaiting prey
Ankles awash in the waves of reeds
Warm mud   nimble water striders   distorted clouds
Nose tip pressing an invisible wall   a deer
That starry frost coated box
Carried evenly on its back   a deer

Inside that deer inside that deerskin, I
Enter   abide   elope
Next morning, I select arrow select bullet fly off
Just then   Tones from a flute float in
(May someone stifle that)
(I say I'll embrace that)
Are swept off to the ends of a current of creatures
Juice of white peaches grown underground   my New Realm
At the ends of the creatures' lives, they lie stretched out
On their backs   the reborn summer   sounds of the grass
Hyooo hyooo   the flute whistles
Stance held, select arrow select bullet   race away

– Translation by Jordan A. Y. Smith

Mongoloid Indeed   Hachikai Mimi
モンゴロイドだよ   蜂飼耳

Slurping
Both hands, placed on either edge,
Drank it up   Over the fire
Roasted   broiled   browned
Lifted up with nary a thought
Between rows of teeth   finally
Meat from bone
Separated
Alone with lunchtime
I was chewing

– Translation by Jordan A. Y. Smith

Friends   **Michiyama Rain**
友達   道山れいん

Friends
What the fuck is a friend?
Flying into sudden piss-fits
When the going gets tougher than you'd like
That "loan" of the extended hand or
That leveraging of a superior position, higher ground,
To thoroughly
Invade
Corralling your psyche
Into the pain pen
I don't need that shit
Fuck no
I love me some solitude
Anyway, I'm always
Searching out something annoying in everyone

But lately
I had a change of heart
People I do actually love
I've come to love forever
The bones and the flesh
They wear
That light stank of the breath
The force of the stories they blow out their pieholes
The chunks of their lunch
That end up on my arm
But do no harm
So I play it off, pretend I'm chunk free
(Then with masterful ninja timing I wipe that shit on the back of
my chair, because hey it is pretty fucking gross)
Play it off
And that little effort

Isn't such a big deal
I let it slide, dude
There's a warmth it in (not in the flying chunk, to be clear)
In their truly lovable presence, the fact of them just being *there*
Their soul

In and of itself, so precious, so adorable, I'm like,
awwww I just freakin love it

For a guy like me
To feel something like that
Even a little
Is a pretty goddamn amazing
Triumph of the human spirit

So what I'm saying is:
Friends—who gives a fuck
Your
Soul
Just happens to exist
In the same era as me
In the same general vicinity
A circumstance wrapped in bones and flesh
Here on earth
Going shopping at a bunch of stores and shit
Today it failed to go, but
Once you treated me to some
Seriously yummy grub
One time I lost my watch
But it wasn't at that store
(it was under the stool at the pub when I went back)
at the bbq place, dude
so many stories, talking all kinds of shit,
once we start,
can't stop won't stop get it get it

just go on and on, motor-mouth style

I love that about you

That's why I say:

The "friends" label,
who gives a fuck?

– Translation by Jordan A. Y. Smith

You're a Person   Michiyama Rain
あなたはひと   道山れいん

You're a person and
I'm a person
That's why we can't connect
Can't communicate

You're a person and
I'm a person and
How can that be why we can't communicate

And you
You spent your day as you pleased

I spent my own day

So nothing flows between us
Though up 'til yesterday
Everything was flowing so well
What happened?
Nothing gets through

Now
Absolutely nothing
Gets through

– Translation by Jordan A. Y. Smith

Afterword   Michiyama Rain
あとがき   道山れいん

The world is ending.
Since birth, I've thought it several times.
But it never ended.
Giving up on giving up, the world continued nonchalantly on.

Eternal youth, not of humans but of Earth
Sadness, grievances, frustrations, strife—all of it,
          As the world spirals,
          Like an atmospheric renewal,
Having none of it, this world keeps on keeping on.

All I can do is
Soak in this bath, sleep, somehow rise in the morning
                              (after an extra snooze session,
          say),
And with this ungraspable mess of somethingorother,
This instability, give it words.

So doing, I too become immortal.
That's the feeling I get.
With absolute certainty.

The rain has come.

                              – Translation by Jordan A. Y. Smith

My Act of Faith:
Review of Jeffrey Angles'
These Things Here and Now:
Poetic Responses to the March 11, 2011 Disasters
Josai University Press, 2016.

Barbara Summerhawk

(Jeffrey) Angles
Right, acute;
Aware of a people's need
To speak out, up, talk story, stand
On the still quaking North
Knowing These Things Here and Now
Give us courage and hope,
Reinforces the promise of poetry
Translated across our borders and boundaries
for a world weary of populist junkyards

The earth shakes
Poets awaken
Greet the dawn with bold new words

The waves broke,
Opened a sinister silent threat
Met by wall facers of
(Extra) ordinary talent

The atomic lie
Melts under the glare
of these artists who stand in for ghosts
Documenting, searching for meaning, protesting, United.
Chant out loud these names of Tohoku, our teachers, our guides:

Wagō Ryōichi Daioshō   "We sweat a cold sweat

over our spirits."

Arai Takako Daioshō   "—Did the school of sardines
see the circle of blue flame
drawn from my eyes?"

Suga Keijirō Daioshō   "Poetry becomes the wings that
help us fly, the fins
that help us swim…"

Ōsaki Sayaka Daioshō   "We need music
We need thought
We need words
Without them
our bodies break down..."

Tian Yuan Daioshō   "The sound of the temple bells
have been submerged
But God does not offer up
a single word…"

Yoshimasu Gōzō Daioshō   "In the shadows of the sand dunes
of Rikuzen Takata,,,
,,,enormous scraping hand, working
before the enemy, coming onland,."

And on and on
We will remember
We   Will
Read it, write your own
Act of Faith

A Review of Hirato Renkichi's *Spiral Staircase*

Kathryn M. Tanaka

Spiral Staircase: Collected Poems. By Hirato Renkichi. Trans. Sho Sugita. New York: Ugly Duckling Presse, 2017.

> *We rise within powerful light and heat. We are the children of powerful light and heat. Our very existence is powerful light and heat.*

Hirato Renkichi (1893-1922) wrote these words in his "Mouvement Futuriste Japonais" (*Nihon mirai-ha sengen undo*) manifesto, which he famously passed out in Hibiya Park and other areas of Tokyo in 1921. While his writing career was brief, with this "Manifesto of the Japanese Futurist Movement," Hirato was one of the earliest authors to articulate a theory of Japanese futurism. By publishing his manifesto and distributing it to passersby in the heart of the modern city of Tokyo, he aimed to join a growing cadre of poets who articulated new Japanese literary theories and ideas that were firmly in dialogue with international literary trends of the time.

Over the past decade, Japanese modernism, surrealism, and futurism have been the subject of renewed critical attention, with scholars such as Miryam Sas, Miriam Silverberg, Thomas R. H. Havens, and Gennifer Weisenfeld, among many, many others, increasingly turning their attention to the subjects. In addition, academics have taken up diverse topics related to modernism and the avant-garde in Japan, ranging from drama to architecture to translation. Of course, literary scholars have also looked at the diverse literary movements that emerged in the wake of the First World War, with William J. Tyler editing a volume on modernist fiction, and John Solt and Hosea Hirata publishing studies of Kitasono Katue and Nishiwaki Junzaburo, respectively.

These studies expose some significant omissions in

current English language work on Japanese poetry. First, they reveal the richness and the breadth of Japanese literary movements in the wake of the First World War. Until recent years, scholarship tended to sidestep literary trends associated with surrealism, or subsume them under the name of "modernism." Second, they expose the limitations of work that is actually available in English translation. The above studies, together with dozens more, illuminate the rich literary world of Japan in the 1910s and '20s, but readers may hit a wall when they want to follow up for themselves on some of the authors mentioned. Very little is available in English.

Hirato was one of the most important Japanese futurist poets, and among the keywords associated with his work is, of course, *new*. Under the influence of Italian futurism, Dadaism, and imagism, among other avant-garde currents, he developed an idea of poetry that he called *analogisme*. This reflected both in its language and its content, the chaos and contradiction of the rapidly changing world. In his poems, he put these ideas into practice, creating a style full of anaphora, neologisms, onomatopoeia, and visually striking blank spaces or foreign words, among many other literary devices.

This linguistic play is precisely what makes Hirato a delight to read in the Japanese, but it is also a formidable challenge to the translator. Indeed, the density of surrealist texts makes not only translating, but reading or teaching them quite difficult. In that sense, Sho Sugita has done an excellent job in making his translations accessible to the English reader while still remaining faithful to the Japanese original. His translations preserve the linguistic complexity of the original to an admirable degree. Indeed, Sugita's translations of Hirato Renkichi's poetry in *Spiral Staircase*, are a welcome addition to the small-but-growing field of surrealist Japanese poetry available in English translation. The project itself is ambitious; his poetry requires active engagement of the reader to give full voice to the semantic potential his poetry contains.

Sugita goes a step further in this translation as well. As stated, translating avant-garde literary texts is difficult in itself, but orienting the reader and providing enough information while not over-explaining is an additional challenge. To catch the rich symbolism and layers of meaning in traditional Japanese poetic forms such as tanka or haiku, translators have resorted to heavily footnoting a comparatively short poem. While such in-depth explanations add to our understanding and appreciation of the piece, they can also confound more casual readers. Translations of avant-garde literary works straddle the same fine line; the translator must be ever haunted by the question of how to give full justice to the original while still making it accessible.

To this end, Sugita's introduction is an invaluable orientation to the reader. He broadly sketches Hirato's literary evolution and the major themes in his work, defining his oeuvre into two periods. This is followed by an example from each period, with the poems given in both Japanese and English translation. The introduction then briefly elucidates some of the techniques and semantic play utilized in the original Japanese of the poems and explains how the translator chose to reflect this play in English. These detailed explanations highlight elements of Hirato's literary theories and give the reader a map outlining the richness of the original, which in turn serves to help them understand the translated poems. The reader will also be able to recognize the repetition, anaphora, and polysemy, for example, which Sugita discusses, throughout the rest of the book.

Yet, one of Hirato's most striking techniques is his juxtaposition of imagery mirrored by linguistic breaks. Consider the following passage from "Four Developments in My New Poetic Movement of 1921" (一九二一年における我新詩運動の四種の展開), a series of four poems that represent different avant-garde trends:

The City of Tokyo draped over the stench of hospitals,
like the Virgin Mary above you praying for the beach

rose-colored sunset the fine asphalt highways I pray for
music of people walking I pray for holding the rose flowers
draped over the City of Tokyo   glorious
stars for people

Girl with eyes in pain a boy wrapped in bandage the little
thief of phosphorescence pulmonary disease beriberi
shiveling shoddy university student—a neurasthenia
sample—you and women frail with no repulsive
force====*kikku kukkokku kuekku kerokku hyara vvvvvv* (74)

This poem foregrounds the chaos of the city, with the swirling images of people disintegrating into cacophony, and the use of italics in English echoing the boxy katakana characters in the original Japanese. Given the subtitle, "Temporal Futurist Poem" (時間的未来派の詩), the first poem in this series marks the passage of time by moving from concrete images of the city to an explosion of noise that loses meaning. Yet, as the poem continues, the images of the rose and of the star and its light recur and coalesce, which allows the reader to create meaning out of the noise. The end result is a profound meditation on modern life, and the way in which we make sense of both the world and literature after the First World War. It also serves to foreground the way in which literary theories shaped Hirato's own work and the way they reflected his lived experiences.

In the end, Hirato's most intriguing pieces ruminate on war, life, and death, through the use of hybrid languages and linguistic play as a means to reinforce his images or ideas. The result is a bold, important collection of poems that has had a small but dedicated readership in Japan. Sho Sugita has made an important contribution to Japanese literature in English with his brilliant collection of translations. Indeed, the urgency of these poems is one that has not faded in the near century since they were written; Hirato's voice and his literary experiments remain hauntingly pertinent and important today.

Review:

Something
Other
Than
Other

By Philip Rowland
Isobar Press, 2016

Taylor Mignon

While Joseph Massey's quotation on the back cover of this volume—"You can't step in the same Philip Rowland poem twice"—holds true, a few of Rowland's poems invoke the atmosphere of Cid Corman's poetry. A friend once remarked reading Cid's poetry is like "stepping into a bottomless void." What with all those abstract nouns and lack of adjectives to speak of... Here's a quatrain from Rowland with only two adjectives:

> out of the thin air
> and in the thick of it
> whatever we might think
> however thin the seeming thread

Just as Corman remarkably often turned an idiom on its head, so does Rowland manage to pull off two clichés. This is a compliment, because Cid's influence on twentieth and twenty-first century poetry continues to be strong—particularly in respect to his role in shaping the genre of the short poem.

From his seminal journal *Origin*, and the championing of objectivism and beyond, to his well-respected versions of Matsuo Basho, Corman's mark can often be felt when reading short poetry these days. Yet when contemporary poets seem to mimic his voice, the result is usually compositions with a poetic spirit devoid of humor and a whiff of holier-than-thou-ness.

Returning to the poetry of Philip Rowland, the first thing that caught my attention with this volume is the title, where the vertical positioning on the cover begs that it also be read as an acronym spelling "SOTO," which in Japanese means "outside," or even "other" (外). The second eye-catcher is the front cover artwork by Onchi Koshiro – "Impromptu No. 1 – Wet Pavement."

Beyond the cover is a page entitled "Vocabulary," where this little gem stands of itself: "where my vocabulary clouds clouds," showing Rowland's occasional self-deprecation among other nuances of humor.

An instance of literal and physical depth and a purposeful vagueness is expressed with: "deep within / the falling snow / a truer word for it" – as though by not naming it, it becomes named.

What sets apart Rowland from the Cormanesque school is his sense of humor – he has a sharp eye for it. "Snow" is an example of a short vision worth a chuckle: "a woman going bald reading a poem."

This one sends shivers up the spine, similar to how a Nagata Koi haiku would:

    dark
    cloud

    some
    sunlight

sieved
over

darker
sea

Among the suite of poems titled, "Night Shift," are meditations on clocks in winter in empty classrooms, cherry blossom petals ("returned to sender") and a hyper-surrealistic eyeball out of its usual surroundings. Some of the poetry is syllabic ("after / love" and "dark / i / am"), there are a few examples of concrete poetry and there's even a list poem, the hilarious "Photos of Poets," seriously taking the piss out of pretentiousness.

One of the most thought-provoking poems might be:

under closed circuit
surveillance

old snow
on an island
in the pond

It evokes Basho with the words "old" and "pond" in a new context. Bewilderment occurs as enlightenment is exchanged for contemporary paranoia and bureaucratic absurdity.

Philip Rowland manages to reinvigorate the genre of the short poem itself with fleeting, nuanced, well-caught deep thoughts; and pointed, outstanding images – while not taking his work too seriously – which adds a rare joy and charm.

Contributor Profiles

Akegata Misei (暁方ミセイ) was born in 1988 in Kanagawa Prefecture. She has been an active member of the Roppongi Poets Society (Roppongi shijin-kai). Akegata was awarded the Gendai-shi Techō Prize (2010), and her first anthology, *Virus-chan* (2011) earned the Nakahara Chūya Prize. Her most recent collection is *Blue Thunder* (Shichōsha 2014), and she regularly publishes essays and critical articles as well.

Jeffrey Angles is an award-winning translator of Japanese poetry into English, having published collections of Ito Hiromi, Tada Chimako, Takahashi Mutsuo, and Arai Takako and selections from many more. He was the recipient of the Yomuri Prize in Literature following the publication of his Japanese poetry collection, *My International Dateline* (『わたしの日付変更線』, Shichōsha 2016). He has published academic research on a variety of topics, from homoeroticism in modernist Japanese literature (*Writing the Love of Boys*) to post-3/11 poetry (*These Things Here and Now*).

Andrew Campana is a poet, translator, and researcher of modern Japanese literature and media. Originally from Toronto, he currently lives in Tokyo, where he is working on his Ph.D. dissertation, "Poetry Across Media in 20th-Century Japan." He has performed his own poetic works in English and Japanese across Canada, Japan, and the U.S., and his poems and translations have appeared in journals online and in print worldwide, including *Gendaishi Techō*, *CURA*, *On Spec*, *Inventory*, and *FreezeRay*. He received one of the top awards in Josai University's Kiro Poetry Prize competition for international students writing poems in Japanese.

Jonas Engesvik is Japanese-English translator from Norway. He has a bachelor's degree in Japanese from the University of Bergen, and is currently pursuing an M.A. in translation studies at Josai International University. He was recently a recipient of Kiro Poetry Prize in poetry, for his Japanese poem "クレインの壺," meaning "Klein Bottle." Engesvik was born in 1994 and currently resides in Tokyo.

Fuzuki Yumi (文月悠光) (b. 1991) is one of the youngest recipients of the *Gendai Shi Techō Prize* (while still a high school student, in 2008) and the Maruyama Yutaka Memorial Modern Poetry Prize (2010). Her first collection, *In this Suitable World, This Unsuitable Me* (*Tekisetsu-na sekai no tekisetsu-narazaru watashi*, 2009), published while still a high school student, was awarded the Nakahara Chūya Prize; her second, *Deeper than the Roof* (*Yane yorimo fukabuka-to*, 2013), was published just prior to her graduation from Waseda Univ School of Education. She is active in television and radio talk shows in addition to her poetry videos and collaborations with artists, designers, and other writers.

Hachikai Mimi (蜂飼耳) is a poet, novelist, essayist, and translator born in Kanagawa Prefecture in 1974. She has been awarded the Nakahara Chūya Prize for *The Quickening Field* (いまにもうるおっていく陣地), the Ministry of Education's Fine Arts Award for New Writers for *The Night the Eaters Are Eaten* (食うものは食われる夜), and the Ayukawa Nobuo Prize for *The Water that Washes My Face* (顔をあらう水). She has published a handful of novels, including *Red Crystal* (紅水晶) and *Turnover* (転身), as well as anthologies such as *The Eyes on a Peacock's Feathers Are Watching* (孔雀の羽の目がみてる) and *The Stone that Pulls in the Sky* (空を引き寄せる石). She also writes children's literature and has translated works from Aesop and Hans Christian Andersen.

Hirokawa Chiaki (廣川ちあき) was born in 1996 in Toyama Prefecture. She writes spoken word/performance poetry and currently studies at University of Tokyo, College of Arts & Science. She began composing *haiku* in middle school and *tanka* in high school, and she is currently a member of her university *tanka* society. In 2016, she began writing and performing free verse. Recent appearances include featured performances at the monthly SPIRIT reading in Shibuya and the bimonthly Chiba Poetry Party (千葉詩亭) and regular performances in/around Tokyo.

Andrew Houwen is a translator of Dutch and Japanese poetry and is currently a JSPS post-doctoral fellow at Tokyo Woman's Christian University. He performed his translations of the prize-winning Dutch poet Esther Jansma with her at the 2013 Reading Poetry Festival. These were subsequently published in *Modern Poetry in Translation* and *Shearsman*. His and Nihei Chikako's translations of the modern Japanese poet Naka Tarō are forthcoming from Isobar Press.

Ishiwata Kimi (石渡紀美) was born in New York and raised in Tokyo. She is a poet known for her lively performances, and has appeared in Poetry Slam Japan. In 2003, she retired from poetry to focus on work and child-raising. Then in 2015, she retired from her professional career to focus on poetry and a new life on her own terms.

Jeffrey Johnson is a professor in the English Department of Daito Bunka University where he teaches undergraduate and graduate literature and culture courses. He has written about comparative poetics, and participates in poetry events around Tokyo including reading his own poetry to musical accompaniment. He is also a founding editor of this journal.

Akino Kondoh (近藤聡乃) graduated Tama Art University, Tokyo, with a BA in Graphic Design (2003). Her work spans various media—animation, manga, drawing, painting—and has been exhibited internationally, including solo and group exhibitions at international venues including MoCA Shanghai; Museum of Fine Arts, Boston; Guangdong Museum of Art; Solomon R. Guggenheim Museum, The National Art Center, Tokyo; Centre Pompidou, Paris; The Guggenheim, New York; Mizuma Art Gallery, Tokyo; Mori Art Museum, Tokyo. She was awarded a residency at the International Studio & Curatorial Program, New York, and has lived and worked in NYC since 2008. Her work adorns our cover courtesy of the artist and Mizuma Art Gallery.

Kono Satoko (河野聡子) was born in 1972. She is a representative of TOLTA, the verbal art unit. She has published four poetry collections, *Watch Clan* (Shichōsha, 2007), *Japan Quake Map—Sapporo Variations*, *WWW/Panda Chant* (both privately printed, 2012), and *Yanetofune* (Midnight Press, 2015). She has contributed book reviews, essays and more to various literary journals and newspapers, and is also active in the experimental music group "Ensemble for Experimental Music and Theater."

Kubo Mitsuhiko (久保光彦) currently serves as pastor at Immanuel General Mission Wakayama Church in Wakayama. He's been married almost three years now and is blessed with two daughters (so far). He also plays drums occasionally. His favorite drummers include Steve Gadd, Hideo Yamaki, and many others. He has translated some pieces composed by Japanese poets (Misumi Mizuki, Tanaka Yosuke, etc.) into English. He is planning to do a Japanese translation of Dennis Kinlaw's *Preaching in the Spirit*.

Kanie Naha (カニエ・ナハ) is a Kanagawa Prefecture native now resident in Tokyo and active in the poetry world. His poetry collections have been shortlisted for the Nakahara Chūya Prize (*Orchestra Rehearsal* in 2014 and for *MU* in 2015), and in 2016, he finally won the prize for *Yōisareta Shokutaku* (*The Laid Table*). He has been awarded the Eureka Prize for New Writers in 2010 and the 4th El Sur Foundation Award. He is also active as a book designer.

Kuwahara Takiya (桑原滝弥) was born in Yokkaichi in Mie Prefecture. After working in music, theatre and film, he began to write poetry in 1994. His first published work "Erina's Profile," appeared in the Shinchō Bunko compilation, *The Poem that Was Born Wanting to Meet You*. He often collaborates with his wife, Kanda Kyoko, a well-known *kōdan* performer. He was the founder of the *Shun-doku* series of interpretive readings of the work of Tanikawa Shuntarō, and has written lyrics for a music project in support of the people of Fukushima after the Great East Japan earthquake. His collaborative book, *Pandora of Marriage*, pairing his poems with photography by Kitchen Minoru, was published in 2016.

Matsuoka Miya (松岡宮) (b. 1972) graduated with a M.Sc. from the Dept of Mental Health/Psychiatric Nursing of University of Tokyo. From around 1997, she began to write poems about Tokyo train stations and station attendants, and was awarded an honorable mention for the Bungei Shichō Contemporary Poetry Prize and an award of excellence in the 2015 Metro Bungakukan competition. Her works combine music and poetry, and she is active in live performance and the production of sound generators. Her CD "Limited Express 383" was released from Athor Harmonics (2014). She has a Ph.D. in healthcare science and works as a mental healthcare worker and freelance lecturer.

Michiyama Rain (道山れいん) Born in Miike Shin-machi, Ōmuta in Fukuoka Prefecture, he is Tonka John (ask him the history behind this!) of the Michiyama Liquor Store, with roots in the Meiji era. A graduate of University of Tokyo's program in Japanese literature, professionally, he deals in words, music, and visual images. His first solo collection came out in 2016, titled *Waterplay* (水あそび).

Taylor Mignon is Editor-in-chief of *Tokyo Poetry Journal* (*ToPoJo*) and has advised on Japan-themed issues for *Prairie Schooner* (Summer 1996), *Atlanta Review* (Spring/Summer 2002) and *Vallum* (Montreal, 2005). He also translated the works of surrealist poet Torii Shōzō, published as *Bearded Cones & Pleasure Blades* (2013). He's currently organizing material for a special book-issue of *ToPoJo* themed on Japanese Beats and Surrealism. He is attempting to finish a project on VOU Visual Poetry with Karl Young.

Minamikawa Yuko (南 川 優 子) grew up in Tokyo and Yokohama but now lives in England. She is a long-standing member of the Japanese literary group *gui*. Her most recent collection is *Skirt* (*Kozui Kikaku*). She also writes in English and has published her poems in UK and Irish magazines.

Misumi Mizuki (三角みづ紀) first drew notice by earning the Gendai-shi Techo Prize in 2004, then publishing her debut collection *Overkill* to earn the Nakayara Chūya Prize, and later the Rekitei Prize and the Hagiwara Sakutarō Prize. She co-authored a poem (with singer Sheena Ringo) for the 2016 Paralympics closing ceremonies, and wrote a poetry series for precision-machinery company NSK Ltd.'s "Sense of Motion" project. Her writings now span over a dozen volumes, with the latest being *Good Light* (よいひかり, 2016). She is also an award-winning photographer and filmmaker.

Nakauchi Komoru (中内こもる) is a Kōchi Prefecture native and current Nagoya resident. His creative life began with university drama club, and he currently works as an actor, a writer for television and radio programs, a playwright, a lecturer for acting classes at an arts academy, and a radio personality. Grand Champion of PowerPo Karaoke (improve Powerpoint presentation contest) in 2015 and 2016, as well as Japanese representative to the Poetry Slam World Cup 2017.

Nagae Yūki (永方佑樹) first collection, *Lonesome Flowers* (*Monosabishi-no hana*) received the 2012 Poetry and Thought Newcomer's Award (*Shi to Shisō Shinjin Shō*). Her most recent collection, √3 (2016), employs the language of trigonometry along with images from geology, chemistry, and machinery. She began writing while studying abroad in France, inspired by Sei Shōnagon's *The Pillow Book*, then returned to Japan to study Japanese literature at Keio Univ.

Nihei Chikako has recently completed a doctoral thesis on the novels of Murakami Haruki at the University of Sydney. She is currently lecturer at Yamaguchi University in Japan and is working on a publication concerning Murakami and literary translation.

ni_ka, an artist and poet, was born in Tokyo. She has published "AR poems" using augmented reality technology, "monitor poems" filled with emoji, and other genre-crossing works to widespread acclaim. One of her AR poems, "Best 100 Cultural Energies to Generate Power in 2012 Japan!!!!!" was selected as part of the *DOMMUNE Official Guidebook 2*. Since the Great East Japan earthquake, she has used AR technology in order to explore and create new forms of mourning and expression that dismantle the boundaries between words and images.

Noguchi Ayako (野口あや子) was born in Gifu and lives in Nagoya. While still a high school student, she was awarded the Tanka Studies Début Prize and was the youngest recipient of the Modern Tanka Association Prize for her first collection, *Kubisuji no kakera* (Splinter of the Nape, 2009). Novelist Suwa Tetsushi's influence is evident in her second collection, *Natsu ni fureru* (Feeling the Summer, 2012), and she collaborated with Misumi Mizuki on a *tanka* and poetry book, *Kikanshi tachi to hajimete no tegami* (My First Letter with the Bronchial Tubes, 2014). These translations are from her third collection, *Kanashiki gangutan* (2015), with her fourth due to appear autumn 2017.

Ōsaki Sayaka (大崎清夏) (b. 1982) debuted in 2011 in the journal *Eureka* (*Yuriika*), selected by Itō Hiromi. Her collection titled *Pointing Impossible* earned the 19th Nakahara Chūya Prize. She was invited to the Lithuanian Druskininkai Poetic Fall in 2015. She co-authored the *renshi, Landforms & Climates* (Sayūsha, 2016), and collaborated with painter Kitajima Yu on the book, *The Leaf in Search of a Home*. She has collaborated with artists of various genres/media and has participated in poetry festivals worldwide.

Oshima Takeo (大島健夫) is a poet from Chiba Prefecture, born in 1974. In 2014 he completed the world's first 24-hour one-man poetry reading performance. In 2016, he won the Poetry Slam Japan competition, and went on to the Poetry Slam World Cup in Paris, where he advanced to the semifinals. He has performed at international poetry festivals in countries such as Belgium and Israel, and has been featured in various poetry collections. He hosts a variety of long-running poetry performance events such as SPIRIT and Chiba Poetry Pavilion (千葉詩亭).

Saihate Tahi (最果タヒ) (b. 1986) has written several critically-acclaimed and popular collections, earning the Gendai-shi Techō Award (2006), the Nakahara Chūya Prize (2008), and the Hanatsubaki Prize (2015). Her work appears regularly in major journals and newspapers, and *Eureka* published a recent special issue focused on her. Her latest collection, *The Night Sky Is Always the Highest-Density Blue* (夜空はいつも最高密度の青色だ, 2016), has been made into a feature film (dir. Ishii Yūya). She collaborates with various artists on a variety of multimedia projects. See her incredible website (tahi.jp) to experience her digital poetry as well.

Satō Ayaka (佐藤文香) was born in Kobe in 1985. She is a haiku poet, with two collections entitled *Seaweed Specimen* and *There Are Eyes in You—Wide-Open*. She was one of the haiku poets chosen for the *New Selections 21* anthology, and served as editor for projects such as *Play With Haiku!*

Jordan A. Y. Smith writes poetry and translates works by the likes of Yoshimasu Gōzō (*Alice Iris Red Horse*), Mizuta Noriko (*The Road Home*; *Sea of Blue Algae*), and many poets in this volume. Currently Assoc. Prof. at Josai International University, he has taught at CSU Long Beach, UCLA, Roger Williams University, UC Riverside, and Korea Univ. He earned his doctorate at UCLA (Comp Lit) and researches in translation studies, Japanese literature, & global comedy.

Barbara Summerhawk is Professor Emeritus at Daito Bunka University and one of the founding members of the *ToPoJo* team. She makes migratory flights to her cabin in Oregon where she stargazes and swims, in addition to participating in poetry readings at various venues across the landscapes. Her co-edited *Sparkling Rain: And Other Fiction from Japan of Women Who Love Women* earned a Golden Crown Literary Award (2009), and she is the author of *Queer Japan*.

Suzuno Umine (涼野海音) was born and raised in Kagawa Prefecture. He is a member of the *Kasei* and *Shin* literary associations. In 2014, his first haiku collection, *Ichiban sen*, was published by Bungaku no Mori, for which he received the fourth Hoshino Tatsuko Début Prize. The haiku selected here are from this collection and from more recent ones published in *Kadokawa haiku* in September 2016.

Tanaka Atsusuke (田中宏輔) was born in 1961 and raised in Kyoto, where he still lives and teaches mathematics. In 1991, Ōoka Makoto identified him as one of the outstanding new poetic voices of his generation. Tanaka is one of the small handful of well-received contemporary poets who has written in unflinching detail about his sexual feelings and history. His early poetry was in free verse, but since the mid-1990s, has been writing more experimentally, incorporating the speech of teenagers, regional dialect, erotic language, colloquial song lyrics, and even mathematical formulas. Tanaka has published seven volumes in his *The Wasteless Land* series.

Kathryn M. Tanaka is a tenured lecturer in the department of Cultural and Historical Studies at Otemae University. She has translated the novella "Inochi no shoya" (Life's First Night) by Hōjō Tamio (*The Asia-Pacific Journal*, Jan. 2015). Her most recent publications are "For the Purity of the Nation: Ogawa Masako and the Gendered Ethics of Spring on the Small Island (Kojima no haru) (*US-Japan Women's Journal*, Dec. 2016) and "Writing Ties: Family, Familialism, and Children's Writing in an Early Twentieth-Century Hansen's Disease Hospital" (*Japanese Studies*, Sept. 2016).

Tanaka Yosuke (田中庸介) (b. 1969), the author of two poetry collections, *A Day When the Mountains Are Visible* (Shichōsha, 1999) and *Sweet Ultramarine Dreams* (Michitani, 2008), also works as a molecular cell biologist in the daytime. Since being chosen as "Annual Poet of Eureka" (1989), he has served as editor of the poetry magazine *Kisak*i. He has also contributed as a Guest Poetry Editor of the Japanese poetry issue of *Jung Journal: Culture & Psyche* (10, 1), 2016).

Tian Yuan (田原) hails from Henan Province in China, and came to Japan as a student in 1991. He soon began to translate poets such as Tanikawa Shuntaro, Kitasono Katue, Tamura Ryuichi, Shiraishi Kazuko, and Takahashi Mutsuo into Chinese, and won a translation award for his work on Tanikawa. His began writing in Japanese, winning a Foreign Student Prize for poetry and the *H-shi* ("Mr. H") Prize for erotic poetry, publishing his first collection, *How the Shore Was Born* (そうして岸が誕生した) in 2011. Until recently his poetry and critical works have been published primarily in Japanese, Chinese, and Korean.

Yada Kazuhiro (矢田和啓) was born in 1993. He enrolled in Shizuoka University's Faculty of Agriculture, Laboratory of Forest Microbiology, which happened to be holding entrance examinations at the time of the Great East Japan earthquake. He has recently graduated.

Yamada Ryōta (山田亮太) was born in 1982. He is a member of TOLTA. He has published two poetry collections, *Giant Field* (Shichōsha, 2009) and *Obama Google* (Shichōsha, 2016). He co-authored *First Dialogue* (Shichōsha, 2012), and *TiP! Serious Diary Exchange* (mynavi, 2015). His works for stage include "Time" (2012, Kanagawa Arts Theatre), and "Suite: Water and Green and Wolf" (Arts Maebashi, 2015).

Kyoko Yoshida (吉田恭子) was born and raised in Fukuoka, studied in Kyoto and Milwaukee, taught in Yokohama and Tokyo, and now teaches in Kyoto. She writes fiction in English and translates from/into Japanese. Her story collection is *Disorientalism* (Vagabond Press), and her stories appear in BooksActually's *Gold Standard* 2016 (Math Paper Press), *After Coetzee: An Anthology of Animal Fictions* (Faunary Press) and *Spring Sleepers* (Strangers Press). She is one of the co-translators of Yoshimasu Gōzō's *Alice Iris Red Horse*.

Publications Received

dada 100: 100 Year Anniversary, published by the Embassy of
Switzerland in Japan   http://dada100.jp/dada100-tokyo
*

Beauty and Chaos: Slices and Morsels of Tokyo Life (2014)
Tokyo's Mystery Deepens: Essays on Tokyo (2014)
Motions and Moments: More Essays on Tokyo (2015)
All by Michael Pronko and published by Naked Gravel Press
*

Snow Bones, Masaya Saito. Isobar Press (2016)
*

Woman in a Blue Dress, Yoko Danno. Isobar Press (2016)
*

date of birth, time of death, pp hartnett. Autopsy (2017)
*

Crop, vol. 7, March 2016, Meiji Gakuin's official English magazine.
Creative writing by students, as an editor writes, "Creativity is
everywhere and for everyone." Advisory editor, Michael Pronko.
*

"Yamamoto Kansuke." 27 prints of photography by the surrealist giant
with a bilingual essay. Published by Taka Ishii Gallery (Roppongi),
well-produced, elegant (2016)
*

Tachiyomi art zine by Ashley Ronning
A6 in size (105 x 148mm or 4-1/8 x 5-7/8 in), 24 pp. Risograph printed
in medium blue on mustard yellow, pink, light green and light purple
80gsm paper. Cover is pink, yellow medium blue riso on off-white
250gsm paper. Printed in Melbourne, Australia. First ed. of 400 copies.
Published through Helio Press. Beautiful gift.
*

Excerpt Review
Fractures, by Iain Maloney, Tapsalteerie (2016)
http://www.tapsalteerie.co.uk

her name means dance
we tread barefoot
on plum flowers
*

7inch Vinyl
Poetic License II: interpretations of e.e. cummings and Lawrence Ferlinghetti set to music with muses Jerome Young, Dennis Gunn, Hirose Goh, Sawa Kato and Mark Wild, 2016, Reign Dog Records
*

メオト　パンドラ (Married Couples/Pandora) by Kitchen Minoru (photographer) and Kuwahara Takiya (poet). Book consists of photographs on one page paired with short poems on the other. Thick book with good quality paper and large, expressive photos depicting people in intimate relationships – families, co-workers, couples. Tokyo: Foil, 2016.
*

ポケットにポエジィ published by Nanairosha. Poems by various authors interspersed with photos and graphics.
*

つぎの十年 by Ishiwata Kimi (2010). Poems+prose published in a notebook-like edition. White pages with a slightly shiny ecru cover.
*

十三か月 by Ishiwata Kimi (2015). Poems published similar as the above. With foil protecting cover pages which are made from thick, textured white paper with cute colored drawing on the front. Poems and painted black and white flowers inside.
*

Sbph pamphlet V. Poetry: "Trix are for kids" – Latasha N. Nevada Diggs. Photo series: "Pee on residents" – Melanie Bonajo. SBPH Editions from March 2015. Plain gray pamphlet unfolds into pairing of photos of women urinating in public, mostly natural places, with text by the one and only Diggs.
*

日本の詩X国の詩：て、わたし　第1号　2017/2
「声とよりそう女性詩人」consists of several essays and poems by Suheir Hammad, Hollie McNish, Emitithal Mahmoud, translated into Japanese by Yamaguchi Isao, et al. Small b/w notebook style with a few drawings.
*

て、わたし　準備号
Brown-paper notebook from 2016 with poems by Joseph Mills with minimalistic drawings.
*

*

「Carillon Street・カリヨン通り： A Journal of Poetry & Criticism」No. 16, March 2017.
Poems in tradition forms and some concrete poetry, prose by different authors. Article about Josai International University Poetry Center's international student poetry contest, the Kiro Prize. Winning poems featured; selection by Takahashi Mutsuo, Kitagawa Tōru, Nomura Kiwao, Hirato Toshiko, Tian Yuan, Mizuta Noriko.
*

Hymns & Qualms: New and Selected Poems and Translations. By Peter Cole. New York: Farrar, Straus and Giroux, 2017. A master translator bringing his translation craft into poetry, and a master poet bringing his poetic craft into translation for decades. A must read.
*

用意された食卓　by Kanie Naha (2016). White book in hard cover containing his signature poems.
*

はげしいゆりかご　by Endō Hitsuji (2016). Small, thin volume with shiny cover. Poems inside....
*

What the Wind Can't Touch: 2016 Southern California Haiku Study Group Anthology. Edited by Naia. Rad *haiku* and *haibun* pieces by SoCal locals and transplants. Get *hai* on Cali.
*

A Transpacific Poetics. Edited by Lisa Samuels and Sawako Nakayasu. Litmus Press, 2017. Essays framing identity of transnational poets, their roots and routes and around and across the Pacific. Stunning poems, some hybrid theatrical/performance oriented pieces as well. Interesting photos, concrete poetry, and multilingual pieces as well.
*

Original Homes of Translated Poems

Akegata, Misei. "Vision of Nagano"『ブルーサンダー』Tokyo: Shichōsha, 2014;
"Listening to the Lovers' Visit in the Morning Rain"『詩客』7/4/2015 (web).
Angles, Jeffrey.『わたしの日付変更線』Tokyo: Shichōsha, 2016.
Campana, Andrew. Published in chapbook.
Fuzuki, Yumi. "My Big Baby, Earth" in 現代詩手帖, Jan. 2012, then in『屋根より
も深々と』; "A Snow of Bone" in『適切な世界の適切ならざる私』 Shichōsha, 2009.
Hachikai Mimi. "The Deer Girl" and "Mongoloid Indeed" in 『食うものは食
われる夜』Tokyo: Shichōsha, 2006. Gathering Ashes
Hirokawa, Chiaki. "The Freeze Returns" published in *Eureka* (*Yuriika*),
Vol. 49, No. 9, June 2017.
Kanie, Naha. Both from『用意された食卓』Tokyo: Seido-sha, 2016.
Kōno, Satoko.『やねとふね マイナビ現代詩歌セレクション』Tokyo:
Mainabi Shuppan, 2014.
Matsuoka, Miya. Bungei Shichō 8th Annual Poetry Award, Honorable
Mention-winning works, 2012.
Michiyama, Rain. 『水あそび』Tokyo: 2016.
Minamikawa, Yuko. "Butterfly" & "Examination" published in *gui*.
Misumi, Mizuki. "Fretless" published in『はこいり』Tokyo: Shichōsha, 2010.
"Splashdown" in 『隣人のいない部屋』Tokyo: Shichōsha, 2013.
Nagae, Yūki from her anthology √3 (2016).
ni_ka. 『現代史 100 周年』Tokyo: TOLTA, 2015.
Noguchi, Ayako. From her collection『かなしき玩具譚』Tokyo: Tanka
Kenkyū-sha, 2015.
Ōsaki, Sayaka. "Pointing Impossible" in her collection『指差すことができない』
2014. "The Terrorists" in 現代詩手帖 July, 2015. "Heaven and Earth" in
文學界 November 2012.
Saihate, Tahi.『死んでしまう系のぼくらに』Tokyo: Little More, 2014.
Satō, Ayaka.『君に目があり見開かれ』Tokyo: Minato no Hito, 2014.
Suzuno, Umine. From『一番線』Bungaku no Mori, 2014) and *Kadokawa Haiku*
(September 2016).
Tanaka, Atsusuke. "Memory of Summer" and "Under the Umbrella" from
Pastiche (1993); "Burying the Sun"『みんな、きみのことが好きだった』2001.
Tanaka, Yosuke.『山が見える日に』Tokyo: Shichōsha, 1999.
Tian, Yuan.『夢の蛇』Tokyo: Shichōsha, 2015.
Yada, Kazuhiro. Hyōka, Raigai: RPG no shigaku (Amazon Kindle), 2016.
Yamada, Ryōta. *Obama Google.* Shichōsha, 2016.